IIIIIIIII 10631143

ARE YOU STUCK IN TRAFFIC?

ARE YOU STUCK IN TRAFFIC?

A STEP-BY-STEP GUIDE TO A BETTER LIFE

DR. WILLIAM R. SAUNDERS

COLONEL (USAF RETIRED)

The Saunders Executive Resources Group, LLC,
PO Box 26095, Macon, GA 31221, USA
http://TheSaundersExecutiveResourcesGroup.com/index.html

Second Edition

ISBN: 978-1-943428-00-7

Library of Congress Control Number: 2017918395

10 9 8 7 6 5 4 3 2   1 2 1 2 1 8

Printed in the United States of America

⊚ This paper meets the requirements of ANSI/NISO Z39.48-1992 (Permanence of Paper)

Photography by Marci Saunders
Brochure Design by Reggie Saunders
Flyer Design by Reggie Saunders

This book is dedicated in loving memory to my mother, Mrs. Sarah Lee Gladden Saunders, my first love and one of the strongest women I know. Thanks for teaching me passion, patience, positive attitude, perseverance, and that a "country boy" like me could achieve if I only believe. Mom, the family is doing okay. We miss you so much!

CONTENTS

Acknowledgments   ix
Introduction   xi

Chapter 1
    Lessons Learned: A Ten-Year Reflective Conversation   1
Chapter 2
    Are You Stuck in Traffic?   17
Chapter 3
    Are You the Best at What You Do?   27
Chapter 4
    The Goal! What Is Your Goal?   37
Chapter 5
    What Is Your Plan?   45
Chapter 6
    Networking 101   53
Chapter 7
    Tell Me Who You Are in Thirty Seconds   65
Chapter 8
    Why Are You So Busy?   73
Chapter 9
    It's Time to Get Up—Not Later . . . RIGHT NOW!   83
Chapter 10
    What's Stopping You from Achieving Your Goal?   91
Chapter 11
    Don't Give Up!   103

Conclusion   111
Appendix A: Chapter Handouts   113
Appendix B: Additional Information   137
Homework   145

ACKNOWLEDGMENTS

I would like to just take a moment to formally acknowledge the people who so unselfishly gave of their time and counsel in helping me to be where I am today and keeping me focused on the subject of one day putting pen to paper. *Are You Stuck in Traffic?* is the direct result.

My mother: for teaching me passion, sensitivity, common sense, good manners, and the drive to stay away from the wrong crowd.

My father: for teaching me clarity of purpose, for teaching me about commitment to community service, about the difference between street-smart and book-smart, and about only being afraid of what I cannot see.

My wife: for having the patience to put up with me for almost twenty-nine years, especially regarding the journey to find my niche and my calling in life. It takes a special woman, and you are all that!

My daughter: for providing that positive stroke, saying, "Dad, just do it." You are a beautiful young lady and I am so very proud of you—we are so much alike. I look forward to partnering with you someday soon. Dad loves you.

My son: for being the graphic designer behind every pictorial representation of The Saunders Executive Resources Group, LLC. Thank you for showing me to the world with style, clarity, and professionalism. I could not have done this without your design expertise and wise counsel.

My sisters and brother: for putting up with my nonstop talking as we were growing up, but most of all for being competitive with a willingness to be an achiever and to make Momma proud—we done good! I am proud to be your brother.

Eddie Fyall and Cordell Jenkins: for always being there when I needed you. We have been taking care of each other since elementary school—there is nothing more precious than our friendship.

Bob Dixon, Colonel, USAF Retired: for always checking up on me and providing words of wisdom and encouragement over the many years—you are a true friend.

My brothers/sisters-in-law, cousins, friends/buddies, military family, acquaintances, and associates: for personally touching my life in your own way, as each of you were a gift to accompany me on my life's journey. There is no doubt our paths crossed for a reason and I am who I am because of it.

Mr. Herbert Dennard, host of *The Herbert Dennard Show* and publisher of *The Georgia Informer*, Macon, Georgia, and staff: for believing in my vision and for giving me an opportunity to be seen and heard. Thanks for our many conversations.

The readers: it's because of you that I wrote this book. As I continue to live, I continue to learn from you—don't ever stop teaching me!

INTRODUCTION

Life is a journey, and just like any journey, we all start out at different points. Some of us are born poor. Some of us are born rich. Some of us are lucky enough to have a family that has enough love to get them through the hard times. Then, there are still others who start out in life not finding the love they need anywhere. No matter where we start out in life, we are all traveling the same road with only one goal in mind—happiness and fulfillment.

As a conversationalist, I truly enjoy an engaging conversation with my audience. With that in mind, I purposely wrote this book the way that I speak. *Are You Stuck in Traffic?* is a candid conversation with you, the reader—it's just plain speech.

I started out in life poor on John's Island, South Carolina, on a small farm, the oldest of six children and the only boy among girls until my little brother arrived on the scene. I like to think of myself as a country boy. The town I grew up in was in some ways behind the times, and like most residents on John's Island, I didn't have the things that many in America had like running water and electricity in my early childhood years. My overall education was good, but not good enough to fully prepare me for college engineering. Many times I felt shortchanged and cheated.

Fortunately, I was surrounded by some very strong men and women. These role models showed me that it is not where you start out in life that matters, but what you do that will determine your success or failure. It is where you end up.

Collectively, my role models showed me that with very little you can accomplish much, and that if you believe it, you can achieve it. For example, my grandfather was born in 1892 and was one of only a handful of black men at the time with a high school education. He read the newspaper every day from front to back—every article on every page. He read so much that he acquired enough knowledge to become a prominent leader in the community. Despite the obstacles he faced as a black man in the early 1900s, he was considered intellectual and worldly. I thought he was pretty smart. There is power in reading.

Another example is my father, a self-made man who rose independently through the ranks of Charleston, South Carolina, politics to become a recognized leader throughout the state. In 1980, he became the sole owner of the only black radio station in the Charleston area—Where People Always Listen (WPAL)—a radio station dedicated to providing blacks and the underserved community access to local, national, and world news, as well as music and entertainment. Like my grandfather, Dad knew early about the power of information and worked hard to ensure that the listening audience could no longer say that they didn't know! Additionally, he was a state commissioner and is a Korean War Purple Heart recipient—an honor he received fifty-plus years later.

Last but not least is my mother—God bless her heart—the woman to whom I dedicate this book. She was my first love and showed me passion, patience, respect, and what inner strength is all about. She showed me what it really means to be a loving and dedicated parent. She showed me what it means to stay the course, to stay focused, and how just plain common sense can get you where money can't.

What my role models all have in common is that they traveled challenging roads in life. Like the majority of folks from my hometown of John's Island, South Carolina, they were economically and educationally deprived. But thanks to their thirst for knowledge, they didn't allow themselves to get stuck. And when they did get stuck, they didn't stay that way for very long.

This book is about making you *hungry* for knowledge, *hungry* for awareness, and *hungry* for reaching your goal—no matter what that goal is—to make a difference in your life, in other people's lives, and to minimize or avoid being stuck in traffic altogether.

Inspired by my mentors, I hope to help those of you who are stuck in traffic to get unstuck.

This book is designed to help you with your life's journey by providing proper guideposts that will provoke thought, a positive mental attitude, and ultimately action—all aimed at helping you to reach your goal. I hope to give you the tools that you need to get up and get control of your life today, right now. If a country boy from John's Island can set out on his journey and accomplish his goals, you can, too.

Now, take hold of my hand, and let's walk life's journey together to our final destination: happiness and fulfillment.

Enjoy the book!

CHAPTER 1

LESSONS LEARNED: A TEN-YEAR REFLECTIVE CONVERSATION

SHIFT TO A MORE FACILITATING PERSPECTIVE

Experiences over the past decade of book signings and conversations with audiences highlighted that many readers recognized immediately the traffic jam metaphor but wanted or needed more answers to how they might minimize or eliminate their traffic. They also took this as a moment to engage in deep, philosophical, metaphorical discussions regarding specific chapters of the book and tended to see the author as a consultant with ready-made answers— basically asking, "Can you help me?" As a motivational speaker and life coach, I particularly enjoyed these discussions.

The initial intent of the original book focused on how to get people to help themselves. Approximately 50 percent of the book centered on readers being able to take ownership of their own issues—on readers being able to remedy their own situations through guided questioning and a conversational style. With proper questioning and focus, the expectation was that readers should be able to analyze their own problems and then come up with solutions. Basically, the original book provoked or facilitated readers to solve issues on their own with minimal guidance from the author. However, this original focus did not always address those readers who are challenged to solve their issues or roadblocks without more help from the author or other relevant expertise, like that of lawyers, doctors, psychiatrists, psychologists, teachers, or the clergy. During meet-and-greet book-signing tours—which, by the way, presented a platform to discuss the book and a physical presence with which to engage audiences—I found myself in the role of counselor, consultant, life coach, big brother, father, friend—and yes, a minister—helping people solve problems. These discussions suggested that my audience might need a little more direction to facilitate understanding of solving its own issues.

With this theme in mind, the second edition of the book, especially this new chapter, focuses on helping more readers (65–75 percent) understand and solve their problems without additional guidance. This presented a major change for me, as I truly believe that if an individual does not want to help him or herself, there is nothing that a motivator or a consultant can do to get that person to change or to minimize the impact of his or her traffic jams.

Although the emphasis of the book is about taking ownership of your life's journey, I do recognize that ownership is one thing but doing the actual work to minimize your traffic is another. The book is still about giving people a process that they can use every time when confronted with life's traffic jams. My father always said that "If you are not dead, you still have a chance." My version goes like this: "If you were allowed to get up this morning—if you were allowed to put your foot on the floor this morning—you still have a chance to make a difference in your life or the life of someone else." These are powerful statements because to move forward from the traffic jams of life, you must first start with your mindset. *Are You Stuck in Traffic?* is about taking charge, about understanding the traffic jams, and then doing something positive to remedy the situation. The basic essence of the book remains the same—to provide relevant guidelines, but with a little more real-life traffic jam experiences, to help readers understand and develop processes to help themselves.

RELEVANCY

From a best practices perspective, the last ten years reaffirmed the purpose of the book—that is, to help people minimize or eliminate the traffic jams of their lives by thinking, talking, and taking action to work through their problems. In this regard, the book continues to function as a living, breathing conversation with the reader, taking into account that the reader's circumstances are not constant. The reader, technically, should not be in the same place he or she was ten years ago, five years ago, or yesterday.

As individuals get up each day, they will never find themselves in the same place. *Are You Stuck in Traffic?* starts where the reader is right now. In other words, life is about where you are and where you want to go. The book is a realistic, ongoing conversation with yourself, reaffirming the original position that the book can truly help people help themselves. The conversational style of the book helps the reader define those things that determine who they are. As a result, the new version remains conversational but will reflect more on what it means to have your mindset stuck in traffic and not so much the physical traffic jams of life. If your mind is stuck in traffic because of what you believe, because of what you fear, or because of what you have been conditioned to believe, then you will not seek ways to unstick yourself. Henry Ford said over 100 years ago that "If you think you can, you will. But if you think you cannot, you are absolutely right." You are what you believe. Real-life traffic jams follow.

YOU ARE MINISTERING

For some reason, I always went on the defensive with these words, even though I truly believe that my purpose in life is to help people. "You are ministering" presented a mental traffic jam for me, especially during the early years of the book. My initial response was to immediately say, "I am no minister. I am for profit. I am a motivational speaker." I continued to respond this way until I met this pastor in Montgomery, Alabama, who approached me three times while I was discussing the book with audiences. The thing about this pastor was that he actually bought a couple of books, walked away to have lunch, and came back twice. During his first and second visit, his approach was the same, and that was to say, "Colonel Saunders, you are still ministering." I gave him the same response: "I am no minister. I am for profit—*you* are the minister." Well, on his third visit, he changed his approach. To my surprise, he was much more firm with his delivery. He stood close to me, looked me in the eyes, and said these words: "Colonel Saunders, let us look up the words 'to minister.'" At this point, I actually got it. I truly understood what he was trying to tell me. You see, with the change in approach, the pastor got me to listen by actually giving me something to think about, to decipher, to draw conclusions from. At that moment, I was able to understand in my own way that to minister is to serve, to facilitate, to educate, to motivate, to cultivate, to plant a seed or to plant an idea— actions all aimed at helping people be better, do better. And that is what I have been doing for the last ten years. I stopped fighting the words "to minister" and embraced the meaning of service. On my ten-year journey, I have met literally hundreds of clergy or spiritually minded people who provided the wisdom I needed to truly understand the book's relevance and my purpose.

The old saying that "the good Lord puts people in your path for a reason" was definitely evident, because I immediately had clarity of purpose—the light came on. If you believe, everything happens the way it is supposed to, in its own place, in its own time. These words derive from Ecclesiastes chapter three, verse one, which states that "There is an appointed time for everything. And there is a time for every event under heaven" (NASB). Placed into context, the meaning hints that to everything, there is a season. Similarly, Ecclesiastes chapter eight, verse six states that "For there is a proper time and procedure for every matter, though a person may be weighed down by misery" (NIV). This misery is our traffic jams. We just need to understand, have faith, think it through, and take some action to persevere. Everyone and every situation encountered during the last ten years was about making me better so that I may serve better—so that I could help more people in a more understanding and sensitive manner.

FEEDING PEOPLE'S MINDS—A TRANSFORMATION

As I have come to understand, life is all about learning. Life is about getting better at living in the moment. Helping people is my calling, and my life's journey continues to shed light about the things that I say when talking with people. The realization is that most of my words stem from my spiritual development during childhood. Most of my words or messages derive from the best book, in my opinion, ever written—the Bible. For instance, in February 2016, I decided to do a book-signing tour at the Marine Corps Logistics Center in Albany, Georgia. Although the base was small, my mindset was to think positively about the possibilities. As a result of going to Albany, I met another intellectually astute, conversational person who actually turned out to be another pastor.

The pastor and I engaged in a pretty deep conversation regarding my testimony about understanding the words "to minister." If we're alive, we will continue to learn. As I believe there exist no real accidents in life, I was supposed to meet that pastor that day. In our discussions, he provided another part of my life's lessons taken from scripture—Ephesians chapter four, verses eleven through twelve. The pastor talked about the five-fold ministry, which I may have read about in my young days, but did not recall those terms at the time. The pastor started telling me that I was doing part of the five-fold ministry by feeding people's minds through teaching and through training so that they may receive and understand. This was powerful. This was another "wow" moment where the light came on.

This pastor allowed me to understand the connection between teaching and ministering. When the pastor left, I immediately looked up Ephesians chapter four, verses eleven and twelve, which states:

> And He gave some *as* apostles, and some *as* prophets, and some *as* evangelists, and some *as* pastors and teachers, for the equipping of the saints for the work of service, to the building up of the body of Christ (NASB).

Once again, I experienced a rebirth—a rekindling of my spirit to serve, to help people. I was supposed to be at this book-signing event. It is truly amazing what we can learn every day, especially from strangers. When blessed with the opportunity to get up each morning, we, as a people, just need to believe that good things can happen when you take the time to do the work. You see, in 2015, I was going through a traffic jam in regards to doing book-signing tours and related events because my plate was full balancing the time required for a doctoral program, my company's viability, and my family. I decided in 2016 that I was going to get back on track and give my book a new push by doing more book signings. This meeting with this pastor—like all the others—was no accident, if you believe and have faith. This meeting reaffirmed my purpose. The pastor reiterated that you don't have to be a pastor or member of the clergy to minister. Every person can minister, whether it be as a parent, spouse, friend, or coworker. To feed the mind is to teach.

I am also reminded that maybe five years earlier, another member of the clergy told me that a teaching ministry is one of the most honorable professions. I can remember this pastor telling me to stop fighting my purpose and embrace the teaching ministry, which is all about service. She advised me to continue serving. Although I stopped fighting years ago, the traffic jams of life continue to place challenging roadblocks to overcome. *Are You Stuck in Traffic?* is a reflection of my continued commitment to serve and to minister in my own way as a pathway for people to make a difference in their own lives.

MY PERSONAL TRAFFIC JAMS

I tell audiences all the time that *Are You Stuck in Traffic?* is written to me. I am always looking for ways to improve myself, to make myself better, to rebirth myself, and to rekindle my spirit. For the last four years, I have been reinventing myself. I literally stopped thinking and talking about earning a doctoral degree and decided to do something about it. I enrolled in a doctoral program. This took a lot of soul-searching because in my mind, I did not want to do the work. Folks, if you cannot get past this feeling—this traffic jam—the action will never occur. I considered myself an accomplished person, which in hindsight was my roadblock—my traffic jam. My gosh, I was a retired

United States Air Force (USAF) colonel with over thirty-two years of dedicated service, no young children, and fifty-seven years old.

As a matter of fact, starting and completing my doctoral degree was a direct result of meeting a mature woman of eighty-three years during one of my meet-and-greet, book-signing tours in Huntsville, Alabama. This nice woman had just completed her PhD in 2013. Now, I consider myself *the* motivator, but this lady truly inspired me to rethink my approach to going back to school. Her journey touched me in such a way that as soon as she left, I started the mental calculations for working on a doctoral program, a program of study that I had been talking about for years but just never got around to. You all know what I am talking about. It is called procrastination—and oh, by the way, the graveyard is full of people with ideas and plans that never became a reality. The good Lord sent this eighty-three-year-old, like many others, for me to listen to—for me to get out of my own traffic jam, to stop talking and take some action.

Well, I took some action by starting my doctoral in May 2013. During my initial classes, however, I started questioning myself—doubting myself on why I started the doctoral program. The rigors of the work and being constantly overloaded with assignments presented a major traffic jam. As most traffic jams are self-inflicted, this traffic involved getting my mindset in sync with the requirements and challenges of a three- to five-year program of study—mind you, this was only the first semester. Once I answered my own questions as to why, the program became easier to confront because I understood what I wanted to achieve and the reasons for the pursuit. I completed all of my academic program of study and successfully passed my doctoral comprehensive examination—two major milestones—in January 2016.

Subsequently, I completed my doctoral program at Argosy University, Atlanta, in 2017. We can talk about it, we can dream about it, we can pray on it—but if we take no action, we have done absolutely nothing. There exist many reasons for some things to never occur, but if there is a 1 percent chance of making something a reality, I am putting all of my energy in that 1 percent. If you really want to achieve something in life, you have to do the work—even with naysayers and the realities of life's challenges. This was a roadblock, a traffic jam, but I understood that if I did nothing and was blessed enough to live, the year 2016 would still come. Time waits for no one. I would be sixty-one with a doctoral degree or sixty-one without. The decision was mine to make. I did the math. I did my due diligence. I worked through the pain and the rigor and received my doctorate in 2017.

This is my living testimony that you can achieve if you have the internal desire and commitment to finish what you start. There existed so many roadblocks to my doctoral achievement—time, money, family time, my business operations, writing the second edition of *Are You Stuck in Traffic?*, and more. For me, the biggest issue is getting started. I am reminded of a poster that I see every day at the fitness center I frequent. The poster reads, "Finishing last is better than never starting." These words give such motivation—just like the eighty-three-year-old woman. Start your program today and finish.

PEOPLE DO NOT BELIEVE THEY HAVE A TRAFFIC JAM

Many people believe that they do not have any traffic jams at all and if they did, *God* would take care of them. I typically got this response from the elderly or deeply religious customers who had no problem telling me that whatever traffic jams or problems they have, *God* would take care of them. This led to extensive discussions on faith and individual responsibility to think and do the right things to make one's life better. I tended to quote, "Faith without works is dead," which is a popular saying with spiritually minded people. This quote means that you have to do the work to achieve. The problem is that most people don't want to do the work. Many times, I found myself saying that "there is no place in the Bible that says *God* will do the work for you." *God* gave us the ability to make choices, to think. Now, I could be wrong. If you want to lose weight, for instance, you have to do the work by changing your eating habits or by engaging in an exercise program.

STUCK IN OTHER PEOPLE'S TRAFFIC

The other perspective that I present to audiences involves a discussion about the fact that many of us are stuck in other people's traffic. We may have done all the right things in our own life, but our family members, friends, and coworkers have not. Folks, you can do everything right and still lose. The goal, however, is to strive to do the right things—to give your best. As a result, we spend most of our time taking care of other people's problems, other people's traffic jams. We stop working on our dreams and spend enormous amounts of time solving other people's problems, putting our dreams on hold. My advice to all of my readers is this—don't ever stop working on your dreams for anybody—unless, of course, the reason involves a moral responsibility like taking care of a sick spouse, family member, or child. By the way, in my opinion, the only true people stuck in traffic are children, particularly young children of preteen years. Do you know why?

Well, the answer for this assertion is that young children usually don't have a choice until they become adults. It is also important to note that as children grow, they become more independent in thought and may not do something just because you as the parent say so. The true purpose of parents, in my opinion, is to raise our children to become entirely independent, to leave home, and to live on their own. The problem arises when we do all the work for our children—when we enable our children by doing too much for them. This same mindset enables others to take advantage of your willingness to do their work, even when nothing is wrong with them physically or mentally. Your children, your family members, your coworkers, and your friends will stand by and let you do the work—but only if you allow them to do so.

MOTHER WITH NO TIME FOR HERSELF

I met a mother who was literally stressed out from having insufficient time to do anything for herself. She recognized and understood immediately the *Are You Stuck in Traffic?* message or metaphor but did not have solutions for her issue. After engaging in a facilitating discussion, I basically asked her to describe how she spent her time, or walk me through her typical day. Well, she was a mother of three girls ranging in age from nine to fifteen. Because she wanted to be a good mother, she washed all the children's clothes, cooked all the food, and basically did everything for the girls.

This mother basically wanted her girls to just concentrate on their schoolwork without the distractions associated with what many of us know as chores, especially with middle school–age children and above. I immediately said to myself that she needed to take some things off her plate. You are probably thinking the same thing. Without being condescending, I wanted this mother to tell me what changes she thought could be made to free up some time.

While she was thinking, my mind drifted to how I was raised. From my mindset, as a child grows, he or she should be taught to take on more responsibilities like washing his or her own clothes, cleaning up his or her room, making his or her own bed, washing dishes, cooking dinner, or preparing a meal. To do otherwise is to enable your child to be dependent, with expectations that Mom will take care of everything. Now, I am not advocating for burdening your children with chores, but when you are stressed out by the workload presented, you should look for ways to cut back on the load. This is just my lived experience and may not work for all parenting styles. There exist no right or wrong answers, but just ideas to help with arriving at solutions. My purpose is to facilitate ownership of the options available to minimize the impact of the traffic jam.

I LOST MY JOB

An example that stands out involves a man that walked up to me and, without hesitation, said, "I am stuck. The good Lord must have sent you because I really did not plan to come to the military base today. There must be a reason for you to be here. I need some help. Can your book help me?"

My initial response is to always provide some positivity to any given situation. In other words, how can we flip the script to make this situation better? As the man told me about his issue, which involved the loss of his job, he started to tear up. He was fifty-five years old, had just bought a nice home, had a daughter in college, and felt guilty for not being able to take care of his family—that was definitely cry worthy. His problem was that he could not find a comparable job with pay and benefits close to what he had been making. He wanted answers—real answers—from me.

I always tell my audiences—as a disclaimer—that I am not a financial consultant, psychiatrist, or psychologist, but I can talk about life and lived experiences that may help people overcome challenges. This particular scenario literally scared me, as I was not prepared to see or engage in a conversation involving tears from a man. I found myself fighting my own tears to make sure I presented a strong presence. For people who need major answers, like this individual, my goal as a facilitator centered on getting him to express his true understanding of the reason for the situation and the need to discuss options with his family, a financial advisor, or a member of the clergy.

To truly understand this man's plight, I had to stop talking and do what's typically hard for motivational speakers, and that is to just listen without being judgmental. I allowed him to tell me his story so that I might understand his emotions and his lived experiences. I could really see the man fighting back the tears as he said to me that he really wanted a copy of the book but could not afford to purchase one right then. In my heart, I already knew what I was going to do, and that was to give him a signed copy. There is nothing like helping someone get over the initial hump of feeling trapped and then seeing that flicker of hope in their eyes. I needed this man to understand that with faith and a desire to continue fighting, he would overcome that challenge. The fight starts from where you are right now—not yesterday. Each day brings us new opportunities that may help us win this battle.

My purpose is to help people feel as though they have options to remedy their negative situation and then find ways to

DR. WILLIAM R. SAUNDERS

take some action. As stated, one of the first things to do when faced with individuals with major issues is to listen—to let them vent and specifically tell you what their problem is and what they have done to remedy the situation. I would also advise you to get them to see that it may take some time to achieve freedom from this traffic jam, and that the optimum remedy is to use a phased approach to resolve the issue. When confronted with a major challenge, relay these words—the only way to eat an elephant is one bite at a time. Don't force the issue by trying to do too much too early. Like biting off too much, there exists a high probability for choking, for failure, or for demotivation. My hope was that he would understand the takeaways and then review and discuss the situation with his family and support system. He did not have to carry that burden alone. Let others help you put your life back on track.

MOTHER WITH COLLEGE-BOUND, PREGNANT HIGH SCHOOL SENIOR

During another book-signing tour, a forty-plus-year-old woman with a daughter who got pregnant during the second semester of her high school senior year approached me with tears in her eyes. Being a good mother who wanted to give her daughter a chance, she kept her grandchild to allow her daughter to finish school. In essence, she put her life on hold. She sacrificed almost four years raising her grandchild and when she saw my book, she immediately recognized her traffic jam and wanted to know what she could do because she wanted to go back to school. She was clearly concerned about her approach to getting her life back after four years of raising her daughter's child. I provided her with my disclaimer that I could only provide from my perspective a lived experience response, which would be using a phased approach to address this issue with her daughter.

The month of our discussion was January, and her daughter would graduate in May. Based on this information, I suggested that she let her daughter know that Mom wants to go back to school. With that, I advised her to put two things on an index card; Momma's Day and her birthdate, which was in September. For example, the index card would say "September 1: Momma's Day." I told her to place this card in the bathroom, on the refrigerator, the front door, in the car, or anywhere that allowed her to stay focused on her goals. When her daughter asked what the date and Momma's Day meant, she could tell her that date would be when Mom took her life back. Mom was going back to school.

The date represented a timeframe that allowed the daughter to graduate from college, get a job, find a place of her own, and basically take responsibility for raising her child. The bottom line was that Mom would help with her grandchild but would no longer be the full-time caregiver. Understanding this transition timeframe appeared to make this mother very happy. I watched the excitement in her eyes as she realized that she had some options amenable to overcome her family situation.

SELF-INFLICTED TRAFFIC JAMS

During many of my seminars or book-signing events, I typically ask the audience a very simple question to demonstrate how we—and I mean *all* of us—analyze situations for which there are no right or wrong answers. In this particular case, the scenario involves a next-day, 8:00 a.m., life-or-death appointment consideration from your location to a big-city destination like Atlanta, Baltimore, or Chicago that is two hours away. The question is—what time are you leaving?

Most people immediately say, "I will leave at five o'clock in the morning" to give themselves a little pad. Now, this answer is not wrong, but I tell them that when they wake up in the morning, I will give them a flat tire with a flat spare tire in the trunk—or better yet, I will give them an accident on the highway with fatalities and all lanes blocked. This accident scenario is real, as the impetus for my book *Are You Stuck in Traffic?* was an accident on the highway with fatalities. The bottom line is that 95 percent of the time, leaving one to two hours early will get you to the appointment on time—but you run the risk of betting your life-or-death situation on a 5 percent chance of not making the appointment. If there exists any possibility to prevent you from making the appointment, the best answer is to leave the night before so that if something happens, you can walk to your destination. Remember, this is a life-or-death situation. You are not going to have breakfast with a friend. The goal here is to get people to think things through before settling on a decision that may prove less than optimal for the given situation. Lack of planning or forethought causes this type of self-inflicted traffic jam.

CHICKEN SOUP OF IDEAS

With this second edition, *Are You Stuck in Traffic?* continues to present a living, breathing, chicken soup of ideas—a metaphor for the many traffic jams of life. The book's message is relatable to the many issues and ideas confronting individuals, families, and organizations today. The conversational style of the book allows the reader to feel the author's presence while at the same time embracing potential ideas to help them enjoy life's journey. The book provokes individual thought and ownership of the necessary actions to resolve challenges. Every situation requires a situational response—for which there exists no right or wrong answer.

CHAPTER 2

ARE YOU STUCK IN TRAFFIC?

H ave you ever been stuck in traffic? Did you ever get in your car and think to yourself, "I've got just enough time to make it to where I'm going," and then realize that you're faced with wall-to-wall traffic and you were, in fact, not going to make it to your destination? How did that make you feel? Were you upset? Were you afraid? Were you angry? In my case, I get pretty frustrated and as a result, start blaming the other folks in their cars who are stuck in traffic just like me. I also place the blame for my being stuck on the architects and engineers who designed the highway. As an engineer, I would have designed the highway with numerous exit points to avoid miles and miles of congested traffic. Did you think about turning back and giving up? Well, I sure did—thought about doing irrational things like illegally crossing the median for a U-turn or backing up on the side of the highway to an earlier exit. Being stuck in traffic may cause you to miss out on a once-in-a-lifetime opportunity. So, the bottom line is that you must anticipate the traffic. If you do, you would be better prepared, like leaving early or better yet, taking another route.

WHAT ARE THE THINGS IN YOUR LIFE THAT HAVE YOU STUCK IN TRAFFIC? AND WHY DIDN'T YOU ANTICIPATE THEM?

Life's journey is just like one grand highway, and unfortunately, many of us are stuck in traffic. Perhaps your life is where it's been for the past ten years. Maybe you're working a job you hate or that you love, but just isn't paying enough to take you where you want to go financially. Perhaps you are stuck in the same old relationships—surrounded by people whose verbal and nonverbal communications not only suggest a lack of interest in what you are doing or want to do, but are destructive to your self-image. Or maybe you are stuck in the daily grind, doing the same things day in and day out.

Many of us have to say yes, we are stuck in traffic—and going nowhere fast. The sad thing is that many of us know that we are stuck and need to do something to fix it, but for some reason, we don't.

I was driving to Atlanta, Georgia, the other day from Macon on Interstate 75 because I had a meeting at 6:00 p.m. I left at 3:00 p.m. because I was going to have a late lunch before the meeting, and that gave me three hours to do it and still arrive on time. With no traffic jams, the drive to Atlanta only takes a little more than an hour. But lo and behold, when I got to McDonough, traffic was at a complete standstill.

The interesting thing here is that I wasn't stressed at all. I had anticipated the possibility of traffic and left early, so I was feeling relaxed about the situation. As a matter of fact, I came up with the idea for *Are You Stuck in Traffic?* and recorded it while I was literally stuck in traffic. You see, I was prepared—complete with a recording machine to help occupy my time just for occasions like this.

Meanwhile, the guy in the car behind me was jumping in and out of his car every few minutes, frustrated and frantic. In my mind, he was running late for something and had failed to anticipate the possibility of traffic.

Twenty years ago, I was stuck in traffic just like the driver behind me. I had been telling myself that I wanted a career in public speaking, but I continued to work in professions that did not involve public speaking because of the fear of not being able to put food on the table. Therefore, the majority of my career, albeit a great career, has centered around security and acceptability. Being a USAF military officer definitely gave me security, and although speaking was involved throughout my career, I never took steps in my journey to become a professional speaker. I didn't even look at the requirements. I was stuck in traffic.

As I look back, I realize that I could have done many things to pursue my public speaking career while still holding down a job. I could have done part-time public speaking until I made enough money to move into public speaking as a full-time job, but I didn't. If I had explored the other options for pursuing my dream of public speaking for a living, maybe I would have gotten my start fifteen years ago. Being stuck in traffic can mean many things to many people, like being stuck in a dead-end relationship, a dead-end job, not achieving your goals, financial problems, or simply not progressing at the pace you want to go. For me, being stuck in traffic meant allowing obstacles like overthinking problems or letting other people's opinions drive my thoughts as to when and how I should pursue my goal. Many of us are faced with similar obstacles that may at the time seem insurmountable. To avoid being stuck in traffic, take the time to explore your situation thoroughly in search of a way to continue to pursue your goal without being stopped by obstacles—whatever those obstacles may be.

Don't let the traffic jams of your life catch you unprepared. If you are finding yourself stuck in traffic, you need to stop right now, think, and collect your wits. You need to analyze your situation and then take the proper action on what you can change to prevent being stuck. Proper action can be based on timing, finances, relationships, family health, and a host of other things directly related to you. If you take the time to analyze your life right now, you may find that you can make some changes that will enable you to avoid being stuck in traffic. You will be able to do the right thing for yourself so that you can be a better person.

ARE YOU SURROUNDED BY PEOPLE WHO ARE STUCK IN TRAFFIC?

So many of us are surrounded by a bunch of folks stuck in traffic just like us—our friends, our family, our significant other, our coworkers! We're just surrounded by a sea of traffic! And what do we get? We get the feeling of normalcy and complacency.

From my perspective, the folks that surround you or the people in your inner circle of friends present the most difficult challenge to what you want to do in life. This is especially true if your inner circle of friends is happy and content where they are in life. Your friends also tend to feel that because they are happy, you should be happy. Being happy and content for them is not a problem until it interferes with your happiness or joy. This is a very difficult problem because many people feel the need or desire to keep the peace by not rocking the boat or jeopardizing their relationship. So many people put their lives on hold to make someone else happy. Surrounding yourself with the right people—people that think and feel like you do—is important to your success and happiness.

I tell my audiences all the time—surround yourself with people who believe that you can do absolutely anything that you want to do. If you want to run a faster race, for instance, you need to run with people who are faster than you. Unconsciously, or sometimes intentionally, you will slow yourself down when running with folks that are slower than you because you don't want to make them look bad. This is not an intentional act on their part because they are running at their pace—you are just not running at yours.

The same is true for peer pressure in school when smart students dumb themselves down to remain popular with other students who may not be so inclined to work for that A grade. We have all been there. Your personality and actions tend to result from the company you keep. If your desire is to be an A student, then you need to surround yourself with students who want to get an A grade. If you can't do this, then you have a hard decision to make. Do you want to fit in or do you want the good grades or both? This scenario poses a difficult challenge if the environmental conditions are not conducive to what you want to achieve. During college, I was fortunate enough to get most of my classes early, so I was done before 3:00 p.m. most days and sometimes before noon. Because my peers and I engaged in extracurricular activities every evening (parties, card games, sports, etc.), I forced myself to do my homework and studies early in the day. I used my time wisely and my peers were none the wiser, as I was always engaged in all activities. The goal is to recognize the impact of peer pressure on your life and figure out what to do about it.

The first thing we have to do is to stop and turn this situation around. We have to realize that being stuck in traffic—especially someone else's traffic—is not the way we should live our lives. It is not the normal course of life and definitely not the road to success and personal satisfaction. The people who say that it cannot be done should not interrupt the people who do. This is a powerful statement because the tendency for most people is to fit in with peers, especially if the peers are popular. The reason for the popularity does not really matter as individuals tend to turn a blind eye to bad things even when they look them in the face. An example could involve riding in a car with popular guys carrying weapons, open alcohol containers, and/or smoking illegal substances. This scenario is real and happens every day, in my opinion. Don't let people interrupt your journey. If you find yourself stuck in traffic, this is what you should do:

1. Stop!
2. Analyze your situation using the worksheets provided in this book and find out how you can get out of traffic. Make it a family and friends affair. Work together to get out of the traffic jam.
3. If all else fails, you need to turn off the noise. What is the noise? The noise is the naysayers stuck in traffic with you—the people who tell you that you don't have the power to change your life, the people who whisper seeds of doubt in your ear by their nonaction, noncommitment, no encouragement, no pat on the back, and no comment. The people who convince you that you are going to fail or question why you even try. You know who they are—your family, your friends, your coworkers, and maybe even yourself. You need to get away from folks who are tearing you down. And if you can't get away physically, then make sure you separate yourself mentally. How do you do that? Don't believe a word that the naysayers speak, and don't let their lack of support be a deterrent to achieving your goal. You have the power to change your life. You have the power to get out of traffic.

On the next few pages, I will walk you through a series of exercises that will help you get out of traffic and back into the fast lane of life.

STOP! Stop whatever it is that you're doing right now and take stock of your life. Turn off the TV, turn down the radio, and put the kids to bed. Find a quiet space and a moment for yourself and respond to the following comments or questions honestly and candidly.

Define what being stuck in traffic means to you.

Describe the situations in your life that have you stuck in traffic, which you would like to change or improve. (Is it a dead-end job? What about a loveless relationship?)

1.

2.

3.

4.

5.

Determine what you can do today, right now, to change your situation.

1.

2.

3.

4.

5.

Determine the cost in time, resources, and money for you to begin getting out of traffic. Budgeting considerations immediately come to mind, especially when confronted with the high cost of post–high school education.

Do you need to spend money on a certificate or degree so you can find a better paying or more fulfilling job?

Determine what is it that you must invest in, in order for you to move forward in life.

If you take the time to analyze your life, you may find that you can make some changes that will put your life in balance or minimize being bogged down in the routine.

CHAPTER 3

ARE YOU THE BEST AT WHAT YOU DO?

A re you operating at your full potential in life? Are you at the top in your field of expertise? Are you the best parent you can be? The best friend? No matter what it is that you do or say you want to do, you need to ask yourself if you're the best at what you do. If you are not the best at what you do, then why not and what are you doing to become the best? As a matter of fact, for those of you who believe emphatically that you are the best at what you do, what are you doing to stay the best? Sooner or later—and many times sooner rather than later— something happens like aging, health issues, technology changes, or that smart kid from Department XYZ that makes you number two, or worst yet, not even needed. Many of you may not agree with being the best at what you do, but I am talking relatively speaking. In other words, if you are satisfied where you are with your life's journey, then being the best at something may not be your desire. I am reminded of a conversation I had with my mother about my little brother quitting college after two years and joining the military. I wanted him to come in as an officer because he already had the college time completed. My mother asked me a very simple question, and that was, "Is he happy?"

As I could not argue with that rationale from my wise mother, I started to walk away but turned around after regrouping and said the following: "I truly understand your point of view as long as his happiness does not cost me any money." You see, to me, being the best is about being able to take care of your needs, and if you have a family, to care of them without assistance from others. When you depend on someone else to live, you are stuck in traffic. Additionally, the person that has to help you because of your decisions to be happy at a level that is not your best is now stuck in your traffic. The main goal here is that individuals should strive to be as independent as they can without support from others.

As my book is provocative, I truly believe in helping people that are giving me their best. If you can do more and you are not, then assistance from your family or friends may not occur. In other words, if you want to get ahead in life, you have to be willing to put forth your best effort—you have to be willing to do the work. However, if you are happy where you are, if you are content with your achievements, I will be the first to applaud you. But if you are not happy about where you are and you are not doing anything to improve your position, I will be the first to critique you. I know that everyone reading this book will not be on board with this position, so I respectfully remind the reader that my purpose is to provoke thought and action.

I agree with the musician Bobby Womack and his song about Harry Hippie that goes like this: "I'd like to help a man when he is down, but I can't help you if you want to sleep on the ground." This song is powerful because it addresses a situation in which a man can get up but desires to lie on the ground until someone picks him up. Folks, give me or others your best—and we will help you get up.

Are you educating yourself? Are you studying the things you need to study? Do you plan to go back to school? So many people say they want to accomplish something, but they are not striving to be the best at what they do. What is holding you back? If you want to be a lawyer, it is impossible to become a lawyer if you never study law—at least, not a real lawyer licensed by a state board. And if you want to become the best lawyer out there, it is not enough to simply study law—you must live it, eat it, drink it, sleep it, and allow it to fill your life. You need to become passionate about law to become the best lawyer! You must become passionate about what you do to become the best at what you do!

DO YOU KNOW WHERE YOU ARE RIGHT NOW?
DO YOU KNOW WHERE YOU WANT TO GO?

Twenty-eight years ago, I was faced with a situation that forced me to become the best at what I was doing—and I mean putting *all* of me into becoming the best. At twenty-two, I was a mechanical engineering graduate of Tuskegee University—*cum laude* (not bad for a country boy from John's Island). I had a United States Air Force Pilot Training scholarship, and up until that point I had never failed at anything. I had always been in the top 5 percent of all my classes. So I arrived at Vance Air Force Base in Enid, Oklahoma, in February 1978, and took my first steps into the one-year, intensive military-pilot-training program.

Within the first two weeks, I was faced with an exam. Now at pilot training, they had a policy that you could not fail three exams without meeting a board. I failed this first exam twice. I was not prepared. Although I knew the material, I did not know the art of military testing—especially differentiating between answers like "as soon as possible" and "as soon as practical," which clearly suggested to me that I did not know how to study properly for military pilot exams. I know this may seem a little confusing because it was also confusing for me at the time— hence the reason for my failures. "As soon as possible" and "as soon as practical" deal with the sense of urgency a pilot should exhibit when confronted with an emergency situation.

For example, in the case of an airplane engine fire during takeoff, "as soon as possible" means to fly the airplane first by maintaining aircraft control. Although the fire presents a dangerous and serious situation, the pilot must keep the airplane stable, and then take care of the engine fire emergency. In other words, if the aircraft is under control, the pilot must take care of the fire immediately to prevent loss of life and aircraft. Similarly, to land "as soon as practical" means to take care of all must-do situations before attempting to land. This means to fly the airplane, take care of the emergency by making sure fire is out with no reoccurrence. At this point, the aircraft is no longer in an emergency situation, but this scenario requires you to land because it is the practical thing to do. The pilot notifies air traffic control, prepares the crew and passengers for landing, and makes sure the aircraft is configured properly and all applicable checklists items are completed. Landing is now practical. The emergency is handled as soon as possible and the landing is handled as soon as practical. While other pilot training classmates had brothers, cousins, uncles, fathers, neighbors, or friends involved with some aspect of flying throughout their childhood and young adult years, I did not—I was once again playing catch-up.

While others would study in groups, I studied alone. It wasn't enough. I had to become the best at what I was doing. I was forced to go back and change my habits and learn new and more effective ways of accomplishing my goals. I had to learn to read the test questions carefully so that I was able to catch the nuances. I had to learn how to study and interpret the meaning of every word related to a particular subject. It was not just about reading the subject matter, but about fully understanding everything—the meaning of every word—to be able to see the page with my eyes closed. I knew that if I failed the test again or any other test in the pilot program, I would have to meet a flying review board, and I would most likely wash out of pilot training school. This would have been a major failure for me, especially with a wife and a one-year-old baby girl.

The pressure was on.

I buckled down and cut out the unnecessary and wasteful things in my life. I allowed myself to be helped by my wife, allowed myself to fully engage in activities with my pilot training classmates—especially as they related to study and preparation for exams—allowed myself to get and stay focused, and worked twice as hard with my new skills and habits. I did not fail another test throughout the rest of the forty-nine weeks in the program, and I earned my wings in January 1979.

WHAT ARE THE ROADBLOCKS TO BECOMING THE BEST AT WHAT YOU DO?

What is stopping you from becoming the best at what you do? What are the roadblocks that seem so immovable? Money, lack of willpower, lack of education, lack of contacts? Many of the things that are stopping us are not real, the result of our personal biases and perceptions, and those that are real may not be the immovable boulders we perceive them to be. The fear of not achieving comes to mind, especially if you have been told from childhood that you will not amount to anything. We need to take the time to analyze our situation and discover what we can do to remove the roadblocks to us becoming the best at what we do.

WHAT IS YOUR MOTIVATION?

When I took the exam during my military pilot training, I was motivated to push beyond what could have easily discouraged me. What motivates you when you're up against the wall?

Is it money? Is it fame and fortune? Are you doing what you do for yourself, or for someone else? Without the right motivation, it is impossible to become the best at what you do. The right motivation is love or passion for whatever it is that you

DR. WILLIAM R. SAUNDERS

do. How do you know if you love what you do? Good question. Simply ask yourself—if you had all the money in the world but had to do one thing for the rest of your life, what would it be? Would you still work at that job, or would you be doing something else?

So many of us do things because we think we have to. Somebody told us that it was the best thing for us or that we aren't qualified for anything else. We believe that if we don't stay at that job or work in a certain field, we won't make any money or be able to take care of our family. What is that called? It's called the motivation of fear. We have to analyze our motivation for doing something. If you are doing what you do out of fear, you are not going to be able to be the best at what you do. You have to be motivated by love. Motivation has to come from the heart.

Make a list of what motivates you. Whether your goal is to be the best parent or the best CEO, make a list of your motivations.

1.

2.

3.

4.

5.

32

WHAT IS YOUR ATTITUDE?

Attitude is everything! Your attitude can mean the difference between success and failure. Your attitude can mean the difference between getting that job, that promotion, the relationship of your dreams, or finding yourself on the losing end of life.

Attitude is the way you look at and emotionally respond to your world, your life, and your problems. It is your outlook. I just love the song by Donnie McClurkin, one of our great gospel singers and vocalists, "We Fall Down, We Get Up." The true measure of a man or woman is how he or she reacts when he or she falls down. Do you want to get up? And if you do want to get up, how do you get up? How are you looking at your situation? Do you only see a problem when faced with conflict and adversity, or can you see an endless stream of solutions and possibilities? If you find yourself with an attitude that only leaves you with frustration, you need to change your outlook by analyzing your current position in life and also comparing your life to that of individuals doing what you want to do.

Take some time to reflect on your attitude in life. What is your attitude? How do you see your situation? How do you respond to adversity and conflict when trying to accomplish your goals?

ARE YOU PREPARED?

Some folks say timing is everything, but when the doors of opportunity open for you, will you be prepared to go through them? If you say you want to become a famous singer, you have to be ready when the talent scout comes. Take voice lessons, practice singing and voice exercises every day, and study other accomplished and highly skilled singers. When an opportunity presents itself, you must be prepared to take advantage of it. You should always strive to improve your position in life, just in case an opportunity comes your way. To be unprepared is to set yourself up for failures that you may not be able to recover from immediately or at all. The biggest failure is loss of income, which means you could lose your physical assets like your home, cars, and appliances to bankruptcy or foreclosure. Bankruptcy or foreclosures may have long-term impacts on your family's financial situation and well-being. The goal is to continuously prepare yourself by doing your due diligence to stay competitive for workforce changes. This may mean going back to school to earn a degree or certificate of training before experiencing something bad like a job loss.

If there is something you need to pick up or if there is some type of training you need to pick up, you need to do it now. You need to be prepared!

I'm not the best at what I do—at least, not yet. I am not the best motivational speaker out there, but what I'm doing right now is *working toward* being the best at speaking. I am intensely studying the arts of speaking and communication.

When I made the decision to be a motivational speaker, I embarked upon the journey to becoming the best—a journey that requires commitment, discipline, desire, and motivation to do whatever it takes. You need to do the same. You need to be prepared! Start preparing yourself today. Here are some examples of things you can do to prepare yourself to become the best:

- Know yourself
- Understand your limitations
- Have an idea on what you would like to do
- Determine where you are with respect to this goal
- Start putting together a list of things you need to accomplish

- o Finances
- o Colleges
- o Certification programs
- o Family buy-in
- o Job considerations
- o Time-management considerations
- o Transportation issues

WHO IS ON YOUR TEAM?

So many folks try to walk the journey of life alone. But we are not meant to walk alone—we are social creatures; we can't do it by ourselves, no matter how much we think we can. So we have to reach out to those around us so that they can help us be our best. Who is on your team? You have to take the time to find out who is on your side and who is not. Please understand that just because someone is family or a close friend does not mean that they have your best interests at heart, intentionally or unintentionally. Sometimes, family members and friends just want to protect you from experiencing failure, so they do or say things to persuade you from trying. This takes me back to my understanding of military strategy and *The Art of War* by Sun Tzu, the ancient Chinese military strategist from the fifth century. A popular saying from the book suggests that "You must know thy enemy and know thyself," and that most of the time, the enemy is yourself. This is about knowing who has your back or who you can count on when the time gets tough. Your most important team member is yourself and how you relate to the people around you.

Who is on your side and what can they do to help you become the best? Make yourself accountable to someone. Tell a supportive loved one what you want to achieve and allow them to hold you accountable for doing the things you need to do to achieve your goals and become the best at what you do. Make a list of the people you know you can count on to be in your corner as you walk this new path to excellence.

Take the time to make yourself the best at whatever you want to be. Again, life is too short. Take advantage of what's available to help you achieve your best.

If your best is a D or if your best is an F, I love you, and you should love yourself. But if your best is an A and you got a D or F, then you ought to be dissatisfied. My feeling is that most people know when they have put forth the effort to achieve something, like a good grade on a test. If you did not take the time to study or prepare for the test, when the preparation required was totally within your control, you did not give your best. From my perspective, getting a D when you can do better is unacceptable!

It's time to stop all the excuses—all the reasons why you can't do something—especially for those things that are within your control like studying, attitude, and doing your homework.

Stop for a moment and analyze your situation. Find ways to make yourself the best today!

CHAPTER 4

THE GOAL! WHAT IS YOUR GOAL?

W hat is your goal? As a matter of fact, is it your goal? Or is it someone else's goal? Is your goal clearly defined? Is your goal achievable? Is your goal measurable? Is your goal realistic? Is your goal sustainable?

The first step in achieving anything on our journey is to know our goal. Whether it's being a better parent or getting a degree, you need to define specifically what it is that you want out of life. You cannot be vague with this first critical step in making your life better. To say you want to get "a job" is not very clear. You need to ask yourself—what kind of job? After you have decided and brought clarity to what exactly your goal is in life, you then need to ask yourself—is your goal realistic, given your age, current financial, academic, or family situation? If you say you want to be an astronaut and you know it takes twenty years to achieve that goal, but you are sixty years old, it's not a realistic goal. You need to assess your skills, abilities, and sensibilities and juxtapose them against your goal and ask yourself if your goal is achievable.

Now, the next question is something most of us never consider. Is your goal really your goal? I know most of you are telling yourselves, "Of course it is my goal." But you would be surprised to discover that there are a lot of people in this world trying to achieve goals that are not really their own.

Let me explain. When we were children, we had the belief that anything was possible. As children, we were not yet infected with a limited scarcity mentality. We could not conceive of the possibility that we could not achieve something. We were free.

In this freedom of thought and confidence, we may have told a parent or an older sibling that we wanted to be the president of the United States, a pilot, a lawyer, a judge, a police officer, or whatever it was we believed we could achieve. Because of their own fear, they may have discouraged us. They may have told us to lower our expectations, trying to protect us from disappointment and failure. They may have suggested something safer or more in line with what they believed was possible for us to achieve. The result? Many of us are pursuing goals for the wrong reason. Many of us are pursuing goals that are the goals of someone else. We need to seriously analyze our current goal and make sure that this goal is truly our own. For instance, I started my doctoral program to improve my position to reach a larger listening audience, especially some of the elite colleges and universities that most of the time require professors or guest lecturers to have a doctoral degree. I wanted to eliminate this point of contention or discrimination by presenting myself as Dr. Saunders, Colonel, USAF Retired. Although Colonel Saunders represents a major achievement for me and is recognized as such in many corporate and academic circles, Dr. Saunders would be recognized worldwide by all circles. This, of course, is based on my understanding of what a doctoral degree can do for one's career visibility. I truly did my homework with regards to finance, family, timing, and the mental willingness required to start and continuously fight to complete the rigors of a four- to five-year doctoral program of study. The requirements of my doctoral program were challenging and many times I wanted to quit, but I remained focused on my goal, my purpose—to help a larger audience of people help themselves be better.

IF YOU BELIEVE IT, YOU CAN ACHIEVE IT!

It is absolutely crucial that you believe that you can achieve your goal. No matter what it is, without belief and faith, your goal will be out of reach. Have you ever noticed that people who believe that they are unlucky always seem to have no luck? Think about it. Do you have a friend, relative, or coworker who holds some deeply felt negative belief? If you look at his or her life, you will notice that no matter what he or she does, he or she always seems to validate his or her belief. If he or she believes that he or she can't get a raise, for some reason—no matter how hard he or she works—he or she never gets a raise. Even if everyone else in the company gets a raise, he or she will be the only one who doesn't get a raise.

What I'm saying is that if you believe something hard enough, you will manifest it in your life—positive or negative. And guess what? If you believe you are good-looking, by whatever standards, others will believe in you also. The flip side of this is that if you think you are ugly, you are. If you believe that you can do the job, then you will—especially if given the proper training and proper tools to execute on this belief.

IS YOUR GOAL MEASURABLE?

Have you ever started the new year with a list of resolutions? Of course you have. We all have. When the new year kicks in, we set all types of goals. We want to lose weight, get a new job, or make more money. But the one thing we fail to consider is whether our new goals are measurable.

In order for something to be measurable, it must have a starting point. As I always say, in my John's Island accent, "You gotta know where you at." You need to ask yourself—where are you starting from right now? Then you need to ask yourself where you want to go.

After that, take the starting point and where you want to go and connect the dots. If your goal—for instance—is to get to the other side of the river, you need to know where you are on this side of the river. If you don't know where you are on this side, then you don't know that if you just move one half-mile farther east, you could walk across to the other side of the river, or you might just come across a bridge. In South Carolina, at low tide in many of our rivers, you can always find a spot that will allow you to cross without getting your clothes or your feet wet. You must pay attention to where you are—or, said my way, "where you at!"

Here is another example for your consideration. You could be lost in downtown Atlanta while trying to get to the CNN Center. The key here is that your goal is to get to the CNN Center, but you don't know where you are. And if you don't know where you are, you'll drive around all day. Maybe you'll only waste an hour or two hours, and then all of a sudden the light will come on. The light will come on and say, "Stop for a second—let's just pull the car to the side of the road and ask somebody, or you know what? Pull out a map." This newfound light in your mind will tell you to pull out a map and find out where you are. If you know where you are and you know the CNN Center is five blocks away, all you have to do is connect the dots. We have to connect the dots. We must figure out where we are in relation to our goal. If you want to be a lawyer and you never went to college, your goal is at least seven years away. If you want to be an engineer and you don't have a degree in engineering, it is going to take you at least four years to get there—provided you have all the prerequisites completed when you start. What is your goal? And how far are you from achieving it? What are the things that you need to do to achieve your goals?

WHAT ARE THE ROADBLOCKS TO ACHIEVING YOUR GOALS?

What are the roadblocks to achieving your goals? What's in your way? Is it you? Is it somebody else? What is it?

Do you lack motivation? Are you lacking the will to move forward on the things that will make you successful? If you lack motivation, you need to ask yourself—why? If this is in fact your goal, why aren't you motivated to pursue it? What can you do to motivate yourself to move forward?

1. Clarify your goal and be specific.
2. Don't get overwhelmed. Take baby steps. The only way to successfully eat an elephant is one bite at a time, and the journey of a thousand miles begins with a single step.
3. Do one small thing today to move yourself closer to your goal.

Are you exhausted? Do you find it hard to take the steps necessary in order to accomplish your goals because you are too tired at the end of the day to do anything else? If you're finding yourself exhausted and burned out, take time out and rest. You must first take care of your physical and mental health before you can effectively accomplish anything beyond the minimum requirements of everyday life. Once again, take baby steps. Remember that Rome wasn't built in a day, and it is impossible to accomplish any worthy goal overnight. Take baby steps and know that you are one step closer to your goal. If you want to become a great pianist, you don't accomplish that overnight. Becoming a great pianist is accomplished one note at a time.

What about procrastination? So many of us are guilty of putting off until tomorrow what we know we need to do today. Procrastination is a dream killer—it puts you in the category of a person who just talks and talks and talks, and at the end of the day has done absolutely nothing, at the end of the year has done nothing, at the end of ten years has done nothing, and at the end of his life's journey has done nothing. The bottom line is that when you procrastinate, you wish you had done this or done that at the end of the journey. There is nothing worse than to wish you had done something—especially when you had the time to do it. Don't kill your dream with procrastination. From a personal point of view, I always wanted to be Dr. Saunders. But there was always something in the way, real or perceived. You see, I completed my second master's degree in 1996 and started my doctoral program in 2013, some seventeen years later. I witnessed several of my peers and friends complete their doctoral programs, some of whom I did not know were working on a doctorate, as they kept this fact quiet. I now understand the quietness was purposeful, to minimize distractions from potential naysayers. The hardest thing for me to do is to get started, but once I get started, I tend to finish. My procrastination centered on putting myself in the right frame of mind to get started. I did not get into the right frame of mind until I met this mature woman of eighty-three years who had just completed her doctorate in 2013. Sometimes, it takes being in the right place, at the right time, with the right emotional stimulus, to make you get up and start the work toward your goal. I stopped procrastinating, got up, started, and completed my doctoral program, one class at a time. Goals can be achieved. Sometimes, you just need to start. You have the power to take action. Don't delay—do it today, right now.

Are you qualified? Surprisingly, many of us fail to even consider the fact that we may not be qualified for what we set out to do. We've all seen *American Idol*. So many young people compete for the same prize—to become the next American Idol. But surprisingly, many of them are not qualified singers—they do not have the physical attributes (in this case, the singing voice) required to be a professional singer. For those who have the singing voice, why do they fail? Because they do not properly prepare—some choose the wrong songs, some choose the wrong outfits to convey their whole persona, some don't study or don't fully understand the judging criteria, some don't believe they can win, and some come for the wrong reasons.

We have to prepare ourselves to accomplish our goal. If you want to become a doctor, you cannot accomplish that goal if you are not qualified. What do you need to do to become qualified? You need to study human biology. You need to go to college. You need to go to medical school—and to get accepted to medical school, you need to have a great grade point average from your college days, especially in the medical subjects. You need to stop right now and ask yourself—are you qualified for what it is that you want to accomplish? If not, what is it that you need to do to become qualified?

CHAPTER 5

WHAT IS YOUR PLAN?

W hat is your plan? How do you intend to accomplish the goals you say you want to achieve? It is absolutely critical that you have a plan. If you don't have a plan, then you need to stop right now and get one. You need to start putting together a plan today.

What is a plan? A plan is a scheme or method of acting and/or proceeding to obtain some objective or goal. If you say your goal is to become physically fit or to eat healthier, then what is your scheme or method of acting? What is your plan? Do you actually exercise? Do you actually eat fruits and vegetables? Or do you sit on the couch watching TV and eating Ding Dongs, ice cream, and cupcakes (not that these foods don't taste good or have value)? We just need to get serious. We need to figure out if we have a plan and if we have a plan, are we working it?

Is your plan written down somewhere? As you all know, the mind can be a tricky place. You may say to yourself that your plan for tomorrow is to set aside time to study, but then the next day, you completely forget because some more entertaining task distracts you.

Don't depend on your memory for keeping track of your plan. You need to write it down in detail. Be specific. You also need to track what it is that you do every day to accomplish your plan. The specifics of your plan—much like your goal—must be realistic. They should not be daunting or overwhelming because if they are, you are not going to like them and you are not going to do them because of the frustration involved. You want a plan that eventually becomes a part of you. You need to refer to your plan every day, making sure that it still fits with your objective.

In the previous chapter, we mentioned that if you want to be a pianist, that goal is accomplished one note at a time. The journey of a thousand miles is accomplished with the first step. If you want to be a pianist, you first must have access to a piano to practice on or at least have access to a keyboard. Then you need to get lessons—maybe even some books on becoming a pianist. And most importantly, you need to practice, practice, practice and study, study, study. You have to do your homework. This is the same with any goal—no matter what it is. You must understand this process to achieve your goal.

In order for you to create an effective plan, you first need to find out everything you need to know about your goal. How do you do that? Study other people who have already accomplished what you want to do. As I have come to realize in life, there are really not a whole lot of new or original ideas out there today—somebody has done or is successfully doing what you want to do or doing something pretty close to what you want to do. Who are these people, and how did they get to be where they are?

Pay attention to their whole story—especially the periods of time in which they may have failed. Pay attention to what they did to pick themselves up from this failure. Pay attention to what motivated them to try again. Pay attention to everything related to their goal and their plans to achieve their goal. What are all the things related to what you do that must or should be considered? Read books and articles about the people who have already accomplished the thing that you want, about those who failed and why they didn't get back in the game, and about your industry and related industries.

Attend conferences, workshops, and seminars that inform and allow you to network with people doing what you want to do. Please don't underestimate the power of networking. There is an old saying that you never really know who you are talking to or who is listening—so when you talk to people, make sure you are on par, and make sure you say the right things. For instance, you should not talk bad about the company president or anybody that matters with other people because you truly don't know who these people are connected to. Sharing your personal views and negativities with others, especially people you just met, is not always a wise thing to do. Everyone you meet or talk with is not your friend. My advice is to think before you talk bad about someone—remain professional at all times.

I have personally received a lot of help, guidance, and mentoring from folks that I just met by just being sincere and honest about who I am and what I want to do. My gut feeling is that people genuinely want to help others—look for these types of people in your profession or whatever endeavor you find yourself engaged.

You must know everything about your goal. Don't step out there not knowing the basics. If you want to be a lawyer, you need to ask yourself—what is it a lawyer does? What type of lawyer do you want to be? A lawyer who specializes or one who generalizes? You must ask yourself—what is your passion? Will you like being a lawyer? How much does a lawyer get paid? How many lawyers are in your local area? How many of them are doing well? How many of them specialize? What is the perception of lawyers in your area? Does this matter? How does a lawyer get a job? What types of liabilities are there to being a lawyer? You should never stop asking yourself these questions. This will only hinder you.

WHAT ARE YOU DOING WITH YOUR PLAN?

Are you working your plan? If the last time you pulled out and reviewed your plan was two years ago, five years ago, your plan is an old plan. Your plan needs to be updated to fit the current situation. I suggest you locate your plan and make your plan readily available and accessible at all times. In today's terms, is your plan on your computer, laptop, or flash/jump drive? The key here is that you have access to your plan no matter where you are. Your plan should always include a to-do list to check and monitor your progress regarding specific tasks. Keep your plan as simple as possible and make sure it is realistic based on the current and projected climate for your particular industry. I try hard to stay in tune with whether or not my goals are being accomplished and if not, make adjustments to my to-do list to accommodate necessary changes. Staying in tune with your plan may allow your actions to become second nature, as you will not have to continuously refer to your plan. Practice staying in tune with your plan.

Many of us have goals and plans but lack the action necessary to make it happen. We can have all the plans in the world—but if we don't take any action, we will never accomplish anything.

In order to make sure that you will take action on your plan, you need to make sure your plan is manageable and normal for you. For example, if you say you want to begin an exercise program, is it realistic for you to get up at 5:30 a.m. every day? If you normally get up at 5:30 a.m. and have some experience working out this time of morning, in the cold, in the dead of winter, and by yourself, then yes, this may be a realistic goal. But if you usually sleep in until 10:00 a.m. on weekdays and 1:00 p.m. on weekends and you can't walk ten feet, then this may not be a realistic goal for you. We need to be honest with ourselves. Is your plan realistic and manageable for you?

I was always told that no matter what, you must run your own race. Don't run someone else's race. If you can't run fast, run slow or jog—if you can't run at all, then walk and be the fastest walker in your neighborhood; if you can't be the fastest walker, just walk. The key here is to work out at your own pace to avoid burnout. Remember—you need to take baby steps so that you won't become overwhelmed, give up, or procrastinate.

Many of us don't take action on our plan because we have bitten off more than we can chew. We have too much on our plate. How much is on your plate? If you are feeling overwhelmed by the thought of your plan, it may be that you have too much on your plate. Prioritize your plan. What are the most important items in your plan? Do the most important things first. Don't put the cart before the horse. And most importantly, don't be afraid to modify your plan as needed. If you are not able to accomplish the things you want in the allotted amount of time or in the order you originally planned, then don't be afraid to change your plan and begin again.

On the next few pages are some questions designed to help you create and implement your plan.

From these major steps in your plan, what is the order of priority for each step, complete with all the minor details that must be accomplished? Break down the major steps into a series of tiny steps. For example, if you need to go back to school, maybe the first step is to figure out which school you want to go to, followed by cost to attend.

1.

2.

3.

4.

5.

What can you do every day to work your plan? Write down the things you can do to work your plan. For example, if you want to become a pianist, you can practice for thirty minutes every day on specifically assigned musical lessons or tasks until you have mastered the art of becoming a pianist. Find the time to fit this practice in your schedule.

1.

2.

3.

4.

5.

CHAPTER 6

NETWORKING 101

IT'S ALL ABOUT WHO KNOWS YOU . . .

When conducting workshops and seminars with corporate professionals all the way down to middle schoolers, I always present a provocative opening statement that goes like this:

> Good afternoon. When it comes to professional development or upward mobility, it's all about who you know. And the only way to move up in America comes down to who you know. This is a fact of life. By show of hands, can you all feel me on this?

The response I get is almost always around 95 percent in agreement with this statement, with some people saying out loud, "absolutely," "say it again," and "I hate that." I then hit them with a bombshell:

> There exist no right or wrong answers here, but all of you that agreed with me are wrong. And let me tell you why.
>
> I know President Barack Obama very well. I know absolutely everything there is to know about President Obama. I know Oprah Winfrey very well. I know absolutely everything about Oprah. The

problem is, President Obama and Oprah do not know me.

It's not about who you know, but who knows you.

And the crowd goes wild because I just opened their eyes to the reality that you have to get people to know you. The person does not have to be some national figure or some big celebrity superstar to know you—he or she could be the secretary, the administrative assistant, the deacon in your church, the little league baseball coach, or the editor for your new book. With this background, this chapter is all about giving you a little taste of networking.

NETWORKING DEFINED

According to Wikipedia, the free dictionary, "networking" refers to a supportive system of sharing information and services among individuals and groups having a common interest. Networking is also a socioeconomic business activity by which businesspeople and entrepreneurs meet to form business relationships and to recognize, create, or act upon business opportunities, share information, and seek potential partners for ventures.

In my opinion, networking is not optional anymore—it is a critical talent to master at all levels of your life's journey. Networking is not a simple exchange of business cards at a nightclub, nor is it bragging about yourself or pleading for help from strangers.

According to most experts, networking is building relationships on the basis of trust that involves a give-and-take. The contacts you make should count for something.

Networking is about teaching and giving—educating people on who you are and what kind of opportunities you want to come your way. Networking is also about giving, which means showing people what you bring to the table in regards to helping them.

Because the chances to achieve your goals in life are limited, you have to literally compete to make goals a reality. Networking is about enhancing your net worth by connecting with others to improve your chances for successfully achieving your goals—personally and professionally. It's about getting people to know you through every available medium—through verbal and nonverbal communication.

For instance, in today's workforce, finding a job is not as simple as attending a job fair or sending out that A+ resume. The job market is very competitive, and people who know you personally as well as professionally may be able to help you land the perfect job at the right time in your career. Networking is continuous throughout your life cycle—especially for business—but I think it's equally important in your personal life. The biggest mistake is to stop networking with others who have similar beliefs and goals. This should help you to learn from their mistakes, and of course, best practices. Similarly, or occasionally, you may want to keep abreast of people with goals and beliefs that are different from yours. Knowledge of different people may help with understanding the impacts different views can have on the success or failure of your goals, especially as laws change to accommodate diversity.

Networking is about building relationships that complement all stakeholders involved—professional or personal. These relationships can help you achieve your goals. It is also important for people to perceive you as genuine when networking. Please be honest. Don't appear selfish or rude or fake. Act like you want to share thoughts about how to help others be better.

Networking is now a way of life, especially with access to the Internet that allows marketing your ideas immediately to a global audience.

Networking can be grouped into numerous categories, such as the job-related industries—music, books, TV, advertising, publishing, theater, movie, religion, airline, fraternities, and sororities, just to name a few. The most interesting phenomenon about these industries is that they all utilize some facet of online social media to network personally and professionally. Social media networking is a fast-moving train, warranting a purposeful discussion.

So, let's look at some of the popular and highly recommended online networking sites.

RECOMMENDED SOCIAL MEDIA WEBSITES

Social media is infiltrating the planet, with literally hundreds of new, innovative sites popping up every day. I wanted to provide a listing of some of these sites to enhance your knowledge of what I found by just using the Internet. This is not an endorsement of any of the sites and serves only as information to help you with your networking journey. Learn the nuances of the social media platforms that pique your interest. The big commonality is that they all want your membership. Here are some sites I use in varied capacities:

Facebook is considered the largest social networking site, and is intended to connect friends, family, and business associates. Facebook began as a college networking website in 2004 and has expanded to include anyone and everyone. Initially, Facebook was only available to schools, universities, organizations, and companies within English-speaking countries, but has since expanded to include almost anyone. Facebook has been the leader in this industry for almost a decade. Users create a profile page that shows their friends and networks information about themselves. The choice to include a profile in a network means that everyone within that network can view the profile. Facebook, to me, is mostly social with friends chatting about personal things all day, but it can be used for professional networking as well.

Google+ is considered the front-runner in competitors for Facebook and has overtaken Twitter as the second-largest social networking site worldwide. This invite-only site has amassed over 350 million active users since its inception in 2011. Several aspects of Google+ are taken from Twitter, as you can find your friends and family, share pictures, post videos, make comments, and follow people—including those you don't know, like celebrities. You can post on Google+ with unlimited words and include different groups of family and friends—known as "circles"—and post to them all separately.

Twitter is a social network and also a microblogging service, making it useful for individuals that lead very busy lives but still want to update their friends, family, or fan base. People can choose to "follow" and "be followed," which means that people can subscribe to a feed of tweets from individuals. Twitter was established in 2006 and currently has over 500 million registered users. Posts are called "tweets." Users can also group together posts by type or topic using what is known as a "hashtag." This is represented by a word—it can be a phrase with no spaces— with a # symbol in front of it. The @ symbol, placed in front of a username, can be used to mention and reply to other users.

Common hashtags are often displayed on a feed to the left of the dashboard.

LinkedIn is recognized as a tool for professionals and tends to be used mainly for business networking. LinkedIn has acquired more than 225 million users in more than 200 countries and territories and is available in twenty languages. One of the main features of the site is to allow users to keep a list of Connections of people with whom they have worked. Unlike the other sites, users can invite anyone—but if they get turned down with an "I don't know," it counts against them. LinkedIn is also unique in that it is a job marketplace and is often used as leverage in job interviews. It contains its own Q&A section that is supported by the community. This platform is still a socially based networking site.

Pinterest operates like pinning a photo to a tack board. This site is the most visual of all the sites, as it is made up mostly of photos that are shared across boards with small captions underneath. Users can post or "pin" on each other's boards, much like the wall on Facebook. Images can also be categorized, and users may follow one another. Pinterest tends to drive a lot of shopping, with more referral traffic to retailers than Google+, LinkedIn, or YouTube.

Instagram is similar to Pinterest as it is a platform to share photos, but mainly candid and not stock photos. It allows users to upload and edit pictures, as well as share them to other social media platforms. The main feature of this social network is the extensive ability to edit and play with your pictures—unlike any other program involving a social platform. Instagram saves time from having to download, edit, and then upload a picture. Two years from startup in 2010, the site had over a 100 million active viewers.

Tumblr allows users to post multimedia content in an open space that others may view, but it is geared more toward writers and bloggers. Users post their content in a short-form blog and may follow others as well. The features can be accessed in a main dashboard where people can also comment on the blogs that they follow. As of 2013, Tumblr hosts over 140 million blogs.

YouTube is somewhat of a social media platform in disguise. Founded by three former employees of PayPal in 2005, and sold to Google the next year, the site has more than 800 million unique users a month. Users can upload videos, which others may comment on and interact with in a thread. Uploaded videos are kept in a feed on the user's profile, as well as a section for where and what they commented on. Users can create playlists of their favorite videos and even create channels that other users can subscribe to. Uploaded videos can be up to fifteen minutes long—unless a person has a verified account, and then YouTube allows up to twelve hours.

Foursquare is one of the newest platforms in social networking and is based off a GPS system. Known as a "location-based" application, users can post their whereabouts at a venue and meet up with friends. It's the latest technology in terms of reintegrating a physically social interaction into how we relate in modern times. Users are encouraged to be highly specific about their check-ins, and can even post a floor level. Check-ins may then be shared across other social networks like Facebook and Twitter. As of 2012, over 2 billion check-ins have been posted on Foursquare.

As a user of networking sites, I must reiterate the need for being cautious when going to sites that you don't know anything about. Do your homework and protect yourself from malware or malicious software as well as guarding against inappropriate material.

TIPS ON PROFESSIONAL BUSINESS NETWORKING

For professional development, networking is a vital part of finding new employment opportunities, but it can be challenging if you are new to the networking scene or basically shy. These tips may help you overcome the challenges presented.

1. The goal of networking is to meet new people, so walk up and introduce yourself. Everyone is looking to make connections, so don't be shy. Don't try to work the room, but focus on a few interesting conversations. Shoot for that genuine connection.

2. This is the time for your thirty-second elevator pitch—tell me who you are in thirty seconds. Practice this so that you can talk with specificity and brevity. Say enough to make people interested in talking with you. Understand what makes you unique and play to that uniqueness.

3. Determine if your potential connection has participated in this event before. If yes, then solicit their opinion on reasons for getting involved and expectations of members. If no, inquire as to why not. Gauge this point appropriately so as not to generate uneasiness.

4. Bring plenty of business cards to pass along to potential clients or partnership opportunities. You may also receive cards as well, so always try to show a genuine interest in the person's card and make eye contact. Make them feel good in that moment and also make a mental note about this person's card—or better yet, write something

down on the card after you separate. Don't just pass out cards to everyone you meet—try being selective, and engage people that relate to your purpose. When accepting cards from others, be genuine with your verbal and nonverbal responses. Don't throw away people's cards at the location.

5. Don't get discouraged if the networking event did not generate a good lead or potential job opportunity. Take the time to ask for recommendations on other potential events that may pose a better fit for your upward mobility.

THE DOS AND DON'TS

DOS

Make a good first impression

Know your goal and have a strategy

Be confident

Start your networking before a crisis

Arrive early

Mingle

Know your elevator speech

Look people in the eyes

Be respectful

Tell them "Thanks!"

Follow up immediately by:

    a. Sending a handwritten thank-you card.

    b. Sending an e-mail: "Thanks for talking with me."

    c. Sending a text message: "Thank you for talking with me."

    d. Personally calling to say, "Thank you for talking with me."

    e. Inviting for lunch, dinner, or breakfast meeting.

Be genuine

Look like you are having fun

DON'TS

Arrive late

Wait to start networking

Be loud

Appear too anxious

Stay in a corner

Just talk with people you know

Be fake

Ask for a job

Drink too much

Be disrespectful

Give out dirty business cards

Overstay your welcome

LAST BUT NOT LEAST—SOCIAL NETWORKING SAFETY

Although there exist positive outcomes from social networking, you must be cognizant of the associated dangers and risks as well. Before you engage in networking activities—especially social media—learn how to protect yourself and family members while on these networking sites and locations with which you are unfamiliar. Don't give out too much of your personal information on the Internet. I used to provide my schedule and location of future activities. But now as a passive security measure, I only provide directly to people I know. Remember what I said earlier, everyone you meet is not your friend—this applies to people you befriend on the Internet. Be safe.

CHAPTER 7

TELL ME WHO YOU ARE IN THIRTY SECONDS

C an you tell me who you are in thirty seconds? I need you to be succinct and articulate—no stuttering or stammering. Be ready to tell potential clients the value you can provide to enhance their services or product delivery. I want you to be able to market or sell yourself in thirty seconds. If you're looking for employment, be prepared to let potential employers know the value you bring to the table—the value you bring to the company. If you're selling a product or you're selling a service, why should I purchase your product or service? On many occasions during my meet-and-greet, book-signing events, I have been asked by potential customers, "Why should I buy your book?" My response is immediate: "Because the book is a conversation with yourself." You have to be prepared for this type of question without appearing rehearsed or inauthentic.

Let's say I'm doing some hiring and I have three slots and 100 applicants applied. I have the top ten applications on my desk right now—and by the way, you made the top ten. You made the top ten, but guess what? Your résumé and your bio look the same as everybody else's. So what differentiates you from everyone else?

It comes down to the art of communication. I want you to be able to tell me who you are in thirty seconds because that's all you have. I'm going to make my decision on whether I hire you or whether I purchase your service or products based on how you talk to me—how well you articulate yourself and how confident you are about yourself and what you are telling me.

Additionally—for those of you who haven't figured it out—these thirty seconds *also* involve your nonverbal communication skills, such as body language, demeanor, eye contact, dress, and confidence. You must look the part! Thirty seconds is a long time if you are prepared! If you are not prepared, thirty seconds is *not* a long time!

DO YOU KNOW WHO YOU ARE?

We need self-awareness. We need to know exactly who we are and what we offer the world. Do you know where you fit? Do you know what your niche is? This is not just on a physical level, but also on the level of integrity, common sense, good manners, sincerity, loyalty, character and honesty—just to name a few. Whenever you are selling a service or product or applying for a job, you are not just selling that service, product, or your skills—you are also selling *you*. You must be able to sell yourself. You need to understand what you offer as a person. Are you always on time? Never miss a deadline? Are you a team player? Are you easy to get along with? Many of us forget that we are part of the package, and we need to be able to tell people in thirty seconds what it is that we offer.

An ancient proverb, written around 500 BC, by Sun Tzu in the book *The Art of War*, states that you must "know thy enemy, know thy self." And many times, the enemy lies within—the enemy is you! In other words, we are usually our own worst enemy. Before looking at others for your problems, make sure that you are not the cause. Assess yourself first. Most of us know when something is right or wrong, yet we do it anyway. For example, we know we need to study for that big examination in the morning but allow our friends to encourage us go out for a night on the town. Because we did not drive our own car, we ended up staying out until early morning with no time to sleep or study. This scenario occurred because of making a bad choice—a self-inflicted choice to go out when you knew better.

With no rest and no studying, you made the possibility of failing the examination a reality. Your friends did not make you go with them. You were your own worst enemy. Don't sell this fact short because this is where many of us fail. Don't just study the enemy—study yourself, study your friends, study your family— and do it on a continuous basis. Remember that each day can bring you something that you didn't know the day before. You have to know yourself!

DON'T BE CAUGHT OFF GUARD

If you are not able to tell me who you are in thirty seconds, then I know the following:

- You are not prepared
- You didn't do your homework
- You didn't study
- You didn't analyze your audience—potential client, customer, employer, etc.
- You didn't analyze the situation
- And you definitely didn't anticipate the question

You need to be prepared. You must find out what is it that your potential client, customer, or employer needs and wants. You must anticipate obstacles and challenges. In order to do this, you have to study. You have to do your homework. Don't be caught off guard!

WHAT DO YOU OFFER THAT OTHERS DON'T?

What is the value of what you offer? How will it benefit the person you are selling it to? To anticipate a client's needs, I literally do my homework or full research on my client's industry and where they fit within the industry. If you're selling vacuum cleaners, does that vacuum cleaner clean better than others? If you are applying for a job, are you more knowledgeable in your field than others? You need to be specific and you need to be accurate. But you also need to do it quickly and clearly. There's not a lot of time to make a solid first impression. And if you want that first impression to land you the job—to garner you the sale—you must have absolute confidence in the value you bring to others.

The most difficult question—or should I say challenge—for me as a professional motivational speaker is determining my value. And this determination is based on what I bring to the table—based on my credentials, based on my qualifications, based on industry standards, and most of all, based on my passion: my motivation for being in the speaking business. You must know your value. You must know that you can make a difference for your clients—even if it's small—as long as it is a positive difference.

For example, if a company has 100 customer service employees and they would like to contract my services regarding a seminar on the art of exceptional customer service, I offer them this:

> I can't change all of your employees, but what if I can get 10 percent of your employees to be more proactive—to work harder, to go back to school, to anticipate your needs, to be team players, to accept leadership roles, and enhance the profitability of your company? What value would your company place on such a return on your investment in my seminar on customer services?

As a company or as an individual, you should always be prepared to answer this question!

CREATE AND PRACTICE YOUR THIRTY-SECOND COMMERCIAL

It's time for you to get prepared.

Write down all the qualities and skills that you bring to the table as an individual or business.

1.

2.

3.

4.

5.

Additionally, make a list of your accomplishments and awards.

1.

2.

3.

4.

5.

Using the information you listed, create a thirty-second commercial. Here's mine:

> I am Dr. Bill Saunders, Colonel, USAF Retired, thirty-two years of dedicated service to this country, thirteen months as the city manager of the fifth-largest city in Georgia—Macon, Georgia. I'm a command pilot with 3,200 plus flying hours, a Desert Storm veteran with fifty-seven missions, Pentagon-tested, assistant professor at Howard University, inspector general and director of readiness/homeland security at Warner Robins Air Logistics Center, Tuskegee University graduate, mechanical engineer, *cum laude*—and president, CEO, and managing member of The Saunders Executive Resources Group, LLC, a service-disabled veteran-owned small business, founded July 19, 2005. My passion is to make a positive difference in people's lives through motivation and personal empowerment.

Now you try. Go ahead, write it out—that's right, right now! I left you lots of space.

Write who you are in thirty seconds. Remember—this is your thirty-second commercial:

Now that you've created your thirty-second commercial, you need to practice, practice, and practice. You need to get in front of the mirror. You need to memorize your commercial. You need to tell yourself who you are in thirty seconds, and if you have children, you need to talk to your children. Talk to your significant other. Talk to your friends and have them evaluate you. Don't be afraid of receiving feedback. If anything, you should fight for feedback—especially if constructive. Then test it out on prospective clients and employers at your next networking event.

CHAPTER 8

WHY ARE YOU SO BUSY?

So you're too busy? Why is that? Why is it that you're so busy? Tell me—what is going on in your life? You're so busy that you don't have time for anything. You don't have time to go back to school. You don't have time to take your kids to Burger King or even to the park. You don't have time to get yourself some training. You don't have time to get yourself into a physical fitness program. Why are so many of us too busy to do the most important things in our lives? "I was so busy today that I didn't get anything done." You've heard that before. But how is that possible?

When we are busy yet getting nothing done, it's because we don't have our priorities straight. We are not doing first what needs to be done. We're spending too much time doing what we want to do instead of what we need to do—or maybe we are afraid or just avoiding the hard work of doing the things that need to be done.

WHAT ARE YOUR PRIORITIES?

What are your priorities? What are the things that you need to do to make your life better? If you want to go back to school, what are the actions you need to accomplish? If you want that great job with great pay and benefits, you don't spend your evenings watching reality TV instead of revising your resume, taking classes, networking with companies, attending seminars, attending job fairs, or searching the want ads. You don't sit around doing nothing productive if you have your priorities straight. You have to know what your priorities are. If you made a list of actions to accomplish in your plan, then now is the time to prioritize those actions. What are the most important steps? In other words, what is it that you need to do first?

This is a great question because many people truly don't know how to prioritize their actions. One way to prioritize your actions is to first list them out. Then, analyze the suspense for each action. In other words, does the action require you to complete it by a certain time or can the action be completed as required? For all the items with a time limit, prioritize from earliest to latest. This will allow you to determine what can be put off until a later time. Once you have done this, you can fit in other actions as you see fit, based on your desires. You can't do everything all at once. Additionally, I would recommend that you create a flow chart to help you visualize the timing. Sample flow charts can also be purchased—or better yet, downloaded from the Internet, if you have access. Using the Internet can also save you a lot of time, but this will require awareness of what is available to help you prioritize your actions. You could also ask someone else for help. Remember—if you try to do everything at the same time, you will get overwhelmed and feel tempted to give up. I don't want you to give up—so please get your priorities straight.

WHAT ARE YOUR TIME WASTERS?

What is it that you're doing that you really don't need to do? Are you spending too much time watching TV? Too much time washing the dishes or cleaning the house? Okay, that was a surprise, right? I was just checking to see if you are paying attention. Yes, we need to wash the dishes and clean the house, but even that can be a time waster—it's all about time management. Some people will use valid responsibilities as an excuse for why they cannot move forward in their lives.

Do you really need to vacuum your home three times a day? Do you really need to wash the dishes twice a day? Maybe some days you can use disposable plates and save time. Is the fact that you need to do laundry a valid roadblock to your returning to school? You need to ask yourself—how are you wasting your time?

If your commute to work is two hours, maybe you can take the train or bus instead and use that time to study or do whatever you need to do to accomplish your goals and plan. If you are not doing this type of time management with your life, you are selling yourself short. It's time to make time management a priority.

Some of us spend lots of time helping others. It is absolutely wonderful to help others, but not at the expense of yourself. Additionally, it is very difficult to help others from a position of weakness. I have always been taught that you can't help anyone unless you help yourself first. As a pilot, let's consider flying on an airplane with a small child and rapid decompression occurs. The proper procedure is to put your oxygen mask on first before putting on the child's mask. The issue here is about having only precious seconds before incapacitation due to oxygen depri-vation. So, if you take precious seconds to put on the child's mask first, you risk becoming incapacitated, leaving the child incapable of handling the emergency situation. Helping the child first might seem like the right thing to do, but in this case, both you and the child may lose your life. Take care of yourself first and then take care of the child. So when it comes to helping others, take a moment to see if you are spending too much time volunteering your services. Spend some of that time on you— you are also a worthy cause. You just may have too much on your plate. In the past year, I have personally reduced my participation in many organizations—albeit great organizations— because they took up too much of my time. This is very hard to do, but very necessary if you want to stay focused and achieve your goal. Don't let other people's time override yours—I want you to think about this statement for a minute. Now, some people may think that this is selfish, but this selfish belief must be challenged in order to advance your own goals. To do otherwise gives everyone else the time except yourself.

Similarly, if you are spending time on things that must be done and cannot be delayed, then you need to consider delegating some of that responsibility. Learn to reach out for help. The sad part is that this scenario is so true—especially for working mothers. I don't mean to just focus on mothers, but if you don't delegate some of these responsibilities, your children or significant other will continue to allow you to do all the work.

Sometimes it's not their fault, especially if you think you are the only one who can do the work correctly and at a certain time—you all know what I am talking about. Maybe your children or significant other can wash the dishes and clean the house—give them chores and responsibilities. If your children are older, have them make their own beds, clean their own rooms, wash their own clothes, and pick up after themselves. Teach your teenager how to prepare a meal that is not too taxing so that you won't have to do it after work. Better yet, ladies— teach your spouse to cook and maybe even how to grocery shop. Let your family help you! Maybe you can even hire someone to do those chores for you if you have the money.

YOU NEED TO FIND THE TIME

It is absolutely critical that you find the time to do the things that will make your life better. Stop for a moment and analyze your situation. If you take the time to analyze your life, you may find that you can make the time to take care of you, your family, etc. Life is too short and again too special to be so busy every day of the week. Take something off your plate today. Learn how to say no when and where you can! If you want to get busy, get productive with your life—otherwise you're going to wake up one day as an old man or woman and find your life filled with unhappiness, wishing you had taken the time to fix your life.

If you are reading this book, you are still living, and that says to me that you still have time to maybe fix something or do something that you have always wanted to do. And you know what? You might live tomorrow and the next day and the next. I have said it before—if you have something to do, determine if this is something that you must do or is it something that you just want to do. If this is a must-do today, then you have to take something off your plate to accommodate the action. Again, it is all about prioritizing your needs and wants. Once prioritized, you can then determine what needs to be removed from your plate.

As I analyze my life, there are a lot of things that I would do differently. I was the guy who always fixed things. I was always busy. I was never *not* busy. My busy life even kept me from coming home on time and spending precious quality time with my family. At work, if there was a task that needed to be done, I did it. If someone needed to go home, I let them go.

I taught at Howard University from '86 until '89, and I had workers there that I let go home early every Friday or whenever it looked like it was convenient on a slow day. And lo and behold, every Friday—as soon as they left—unscheduled events started immediately, and I found myself all of a sudden so busy doing their work, answering the phones, and taking care of walk-in customers. Administrative work can be time consuming and taxing, especially when you have your own responsibilities to complete—my hat's off to all administrative employees. I eventually ended up with elevated—well, *high*—blood pressure, which was a wake-up call that made me say, "Guess what? I'm going home today—you guys stay." I took time to relax, go to the gym, hit the track, visit the sauna, and you know what? It felt good—and my blood pressure went back to a normal range. Life is all about prioritizing your activities and making time for yourself.

At that time, I prioritized work stuff, but not my personal life. If life has you so busy that you don't have time for your children, your significant other, or your friends simply because you're trying to get to that next level in your job, career, or because you're chasing fortune and fame, you have to realize that your life needs reprioritizing—that your life needs to be about living.

Although making money is a major issue for many individuals and families, that is not what life is about. Life is about the things that cannot be bought or sold—love, family, and happiness.

Take an inventory of your life right now. Pull out pen and paper and write down everything you do each day. Brainstorm this list—don't try to analyze this list right now—just get it down on paper. Don't shortchange yourself, either. Include everything you do, even the distractions.

1.

2.

3.

4.

5.

6.

7.

8.

9.

10.

From the list of things you do every day, write down how you can eliminate, delegate, or minimize time spent on these things.

1.

2.

3.

4.

5.

6.

7.

8.

9.

10.

Now, write down a list of things that are time wasters in your life.

1.

2.

3.

4.

5.

6.

7.

8.

9.

10.

From this list, write down how you will eliminate, minimize, or delegate these time wasters.

1.

2.

3.

4.

5.

6.

7.

8.

9.

10.

CHAPTER 9

IT'S TIME TO GET UP—NOT LATER . . . RIGHT NOW!

I t is time to get up right now! Why are so many of us still sitting down, not achieving our goals in life? We need to be getting up and doing the right things to make our lives better—no more procrastination. No more sitting on yesterday's laurels. It's time to make that goal a reality.

Procrastination is such a common term that many of us don't know we are doing it. I have to admit—however—that many of us know when we are procrastinating. Many times, procrastination occurs because we fail to prioritize. As a result, we just do what comes to mind first or do what feels better for the moment.

For example, while writing the second edition of this book, I knew the targeted suspense for getting my revised comments back to the editor, but I was also working on my doctoral dissertation and preparing for meet-and-greet book-signing events—as well as family time and "me" time. I tended to look at the other things as more of a priority because of the emphasis I placed on their importance.

To meet the designated suspense, I always place a self-imposed deadline to get things done that is earlier than the actual suspense. With much discipline, my procrastination is then based on this new suspense—which allows me to always complete my deliverables within the original target time. This technique works well for me. You may want to come up with your own ideas on how to minimize procrastination in your life.

In my opinion, procrastination can derive from many reasons, including fear of failure, fear of success, a wait-and-see attitude that tomorrow will be better, caring about the opinions of others, and the sense that you have more time. Although this list of reasons is not all-inclusive, I believe the way to fight pro-crastination is to first acknowledge these reasons, followed by taking the necessary action to minimize the impact on achieving the goal. The bottom line still centers on the ability to prioritize and then execute based on the realities of what is on your plate.

GOD ACCEPTS U-TURNS

If you find yourself going in the wrong direction, stop and turn around. I was driving down Interstate 75 Southbound coming from Macon, Georgia, to Warner Robins, Georgia, and there was a big sign in big, black-and-white lettering on the side of the road that said, "If you find yourself going in the wrong direction, God accepts U-turns." Everything I see or hear every day is an opportunity to enhance myself professionally and socially—just like this sign.

I'm saying to you that if you find yourself going in the wrong direction, you need to stop. You need to stop right now and turn yourself around. If you know that you're doing the wrong thing and it's going to get you nothing—it's going to bring you no value—then it's time to stop. If you know you need some education—if you know you need a certificate to do your job—then it's time to go get that certificate. The goal you want will not be achieved if you continue on the track that's taking you nowhere. It's time to put your life in order. So many of us are going in the wrong direction and refuse to make a U-turn. You don't have to continue on the wrong path. We all have a chance to turn around.

Additionally, many of us allow ourselves to get caught up in the past—past mistakes, past failures, and past hurts. Although you can learn from the past, you need to stop operating in the past. I have had discussions with clients and all they wanted to do was talk about yesterday—not right now, not tomorrow. The entire conversation centered on some event from the past that totally consumed their time. Even when others have moved on— especially with regards to relationship events—they are still stuck in the past. When asked about what they want to do about it, they could not tell you. The amazing thing is that many of them could not even remember the actual event for which they were so passionately engaged. It is important to note, however, that some past events run so deep in people's minds that it is difficult to let go. I try to let people know that they are not being asked to forget but to remember, learn from the experience, and move forward. This moving forward is situational, as each individual responds differently to emotional events in their lives. Death of a loved one comes to mind. People grieve differently and some may never get over a death. The inability to get over death may prevent one from moving forward with life. Today is what you have the power to control. You can't fix yesterday and no matter how hard you try, you can't change it.

When I first started out in the speaking business, I mistakenly believed that people would hire me as a speaker simply on the merits of my past accomplishments as a colonel in the military and as the chief administration officer for the great city of Macon, Georgia. So when after four months of being in business, the phone wasn't ringing and I wasn't getting the jobs that I thought I should, I got frustrated. I couldn't figure out why folks weren't responding the way I had envisioned. Whatever the reasons, I needed to do some more homework. By studying the people who were doing the things that I wanted to do, I learned what I needed to do to be successful in my public speaking career. My involvement and subsequent membership with the National Speakers Association (NSA) and the local NSA chapter definitely contributed to my understanding of what it takes to become a successful public speaker.

I realized that people wanted to see my work as a speaker. I had made a mistake. I spent four months pursuing a speaking career with my priorities in the wrong order. I didn't have a portfolio or a proper track record as a speaker. So what did I do? Well, I didn't stop and give up just because I had made a mistake and spent four months going in the wrong direction. When I realized that I was going in the wrong direction, I didn't despair over the past. I stopped, checked my life map, got good directions, and then turned around so that I could begin heading in the right direction.

I began to go out and speak for free to create a portfolio and a public speaking track record. Every opportunity I had to do a speaking engagement, I did. After being interviewed for a local TV show, I was given a chance to come back and do a weekly four- to five-minute motivational TV series on the subject of my choosing—this was supposed to last for two to three weeks. Well, it lasted almost five months and gave me additional visibility in the community.

You never know what's going to happen for you unless you put yourself out there to be seen and heard. I got a chance to meet some local videographers and as a result, I was able to produce some CDs and DVDs. And by the way, I began writing this book! I got out there and connected to the people that I saw accomplishing the things that I wanted to do. And I'm suggesting to you that you do the same. Don't let past errors stop you. Seize today and move in the right direction. Focus on the things that are within your control.

FOCUS ON THE 1 PERCENT

You want to achieve a goal and somebody is telling you that it's not possible. A lot of people—maybe as high as 99 percent— say that what you want is not a possibility. As a matter of fact, most individuals are telling you that you have a slim chance of success. I have believed for a long time that if there is a 1 percent chance of making something happen, put all of your energy into that 1 percent. Don't spend all of your energy on that 99 percent chance that it won't happen. Put all of your energy into doing the things that can make that 1 percent chance a reality.

As I mentioned earlier, I'm a country boy. John's Island was not a rich place by any stretch of the imagination, but I surely enjoyed those days. As I reflect back, we—the black community—were economically deprived and educationally deprived, at least on a national exposure level, with many of us working on the farms and in the fields to make ends meet. But you know what? I didn't realize we were economically or educationally deprived because I was surrounded by a community of people that lived and looked just like me and were not exposed to anything different.

I didn't realize that we were economically and educationally deprived until I started reading and *wow*, do I love to read. My grandfather loved to read and his worldliness earned him respect as a community leader. This same love for reading exposed me to world events and put a hunger in me to improve my position in life—to work hard to reach a position in America where I could make a difference in people's lives. Additionally, this love put a hunger in me to achieve financial security—to take care of my family and to avoid the pitfalls of drugs, crime, and that defeatist mentality that captured the attention of so many economically deprived youth, especially black males.

This awareness—this exposure through reading—showed me exactly where I did not want to be; no jail, no drugs, and definitely not working hard every day, living from paycheck to paycheck. I promised myself that I would always strive to be near the top with anything I was involved with—I made sure I stood out in the crowd. I was the oldest of six kids and I promised my mother that I would make her proud—I feel in my heart of hearts that I accomplished this task. Growing up economically deprived on John's Island could have made it very easy to go down the wrong road of life—y'all know what I am talking about!

Although many families were strong and successful in their own right, despite the obstacles they faced, I saw most folks working hard all their lives for little more than the minimum amount of money that was needed to survive.

In my own case, after graduating from high school, I began working for a local factory during the summer months. It was hard work, but I could make a lot of money working overtime and double time. I was often working sixteen to twenty-hour days, but that meant a lot of money for a poor kid living on John's Island. I saw many of my friends settle for that life—but I knew that was not my path. I knew that this life was not for me.

So I decided I was going to go to college and become an engineer. I was told it wasn't possible—"it ain't no way you can be an engineer"—this was 1972. But I didn't care what they thought. I knew what I wanted for my life. I knew what I *didn't* want. I went on to Tuskegee University, worked hard in my studies, and earned my engineering degree and graduated with honors—*cum laude*.

But how many people have been told by others that they couldn't accomplish a particular goal? How many times did they hear, "That's not possible"? How many today—as grown adults—are allowing themselves to be kept down by the words of naysayers? Stop surrounding yourself with the 99 percent who don't believe in your abilities. Focus on the 1 percent.

Stop! Take the time now to analyze your situation and figure out what is keeping you down. Provide responses to the following questions:

What are the things from the past or the thoughts and beliefs you hold that are keeping you from moving forward?

1.

2.

3.

4

5.

6.

7.

8.

9.

10.

If you are going in the wrong direction, what are the things that you need to do today to make a U-turn and head in the right direction?

1.

2.

3.

4.

5.

6.

7.

8.

9.

10.

WHAT'S STOPPING YOU FROM ACHIEVING YOUR GOAL?

W hat is stopping you from achieving your goal? Is it your friends? Is it peer pressure? Is it your family? Is it you?

Sometimes what we think is a roadblock is really not the actual roadblock. The actual roadblock is something entirely different. You must take the time to study the whole problem—not just the parts where you think the issue is located.

Start with the whole problem and work toward identifying the root cause. Identify the things under your control that are stopping you from achieving your goals. If you want to start a physical fitness program, what's stopping you? Don't you know that you actually have the power to get up early and exercise—it may only require that you set your alarm? You also have the power to go to the gym or visit the local area track. You may be pleasantly surprised at how many people are on the local track in the early morning hours—let these newfound fitness mates be your motivators. You have the power to take the steps necessary to achieve your goals. If we look closer, we will realize that it is usually ourselves who are stopping our achievement.

It is our mentality that is stopping us from achieving our goal. I've said this before—you need to know your enemy, and you need to know yourself. A lot of times the enemy lies within—the enemy is you. Sometimes we are our own worst enemy. If you are your worst enemy, if you are the roadblock to achieving your goal, then you know exactly what I am going to say—stop, analyze your situation, and fix it right now!

MENTAL BARRIERS

Lack of Desire—Some of us say we want to accomplish this, we want to accomplish that, we want to be this type of career person—but we lack a true desire. Desire is the first step to accomplishing your goal. Without desire, we have no motivation to move forward when the going gets tough. What is desire? I would define desire at its root as love. Desire is a love for something or someone that is deeply rooted and immovable. Desire is the foundation of all great accomplishments. When I was in flight school and I failed the first exam twice, I could have easily given up, but I didn't because of desire—not only my own desire, but the desire of my family to see me succeed: the desire of my wife to make sure I succeeded, the desire of my wife to make sure I stayed focused on the goal, and her desire to help me study and study correctly. It is safe to say that this desire helped me keep going.

Desire is like motivation. It comes from within. I wanted to be a pilot and my family knew this. As a result, I received major family support to make this desire to earn my pilot wings a reality. Although my family did benefit from me fulfilling my desire, the desire was mine to achieve. Having the right support structure is vital to accomplishing one's personal goals in life. Once you have determined your desires and not the desires pushed on you by others, seek avenues available to help you develop this desire. Once you have it, you must do whatever you need to do to keep this desire burning and burning brightly. As parents, develop this desire in children early by understanding their capabilities—along with your ability to facilitate the outcome. Monitor your children continuously as they grow for deviations in their desires and adjust accordingly.

Lack of Faith—Do you believe that you can accomplish what you're doing? As I mentioned earlier, faith is absolutely essential to you achieving your goal. Why would anyone move toward a goal that they didn't believe they could accomplish? Well, the answer is they would not unless coerced or forced to do so. You need to ask yourself if you lack the faith in your abilities to accomplish the goals that you desire. If you do lack faith, take the time to find out why—and then change your mindset.

Without faith, I would not have been able to earn my bachelor's degree in mechanical engineering. Without faith, I would not have graduated from undergraduate pilot training. I would not have been able to fly fast jets in all kinds of weather—navigating by instruments *only* because you can't see outside the cockpit (in other words, you can't see the ground). It's only through faith in these instruments, faith in a higher power, faith in God, and faith in my own abilities that I could fly under these conditions.

We were taught to believe our instruments—this takes a lot of faith, especially when your body, your mind, your sense of balance, and your equilibrium want to tell you something different. For example, when your body says you are flying upside down, but the instruments say you are right side up—which do you believe? Putting your faith in the wrong thing at the wrong time—with not much margin for error—could be catastrophic or even deadly.

You must have faith and this faith comes from continuous training. This faith comes from believing—believing in yourself, believing in others, believing in your instruments. This faith comes from doing your homework, studying, networking with folks that do what you do; and, I almost missed a *biggie*—this faith comes from practice, sometimes years of it.

It's the type of practice that ensures that your faith will never waver when challenged by forces or events that could destroy you. Practice makes your faith strong. As a pilot, I was taught to believe in my instruments, even when my body was telling me something else. You see, when flying in instrument conditions where you can't see outside the cockpit of the aircraft, the only thing the pilot has is the instruments to tell whether you are turning, going up or down, and your speed. On many occasions when flying in bad weather, your body's equilibrium will tell you something different than what the instruments are showing you. It's kind of like getting off a merry-go-round and the body still feels like you are turning. When you try to correct this turning feeling, you stumble or fall down. Well, in the airplane, the pilot must resist what the body feels and believe the instruments. To do otherwise is to cause loss of life or aircraft. When you practice flying in the weather enough, this becomes second nature to pilots, so the feeling goes away. The only way to beat this feeling is with continuous practice. Continuous practice keeps your faith strong. Practice will bring you success. Without faith, I would not have written this book. Without faith, I would not have even started writing this book after being stuck in traffic for four months because I was going in the wrong direction trying to accomplish my goal to become a public speaker. Without faith, I would not have recognized that I could make a U-turn and get moving in the right direction. Without faith, you will not be able to get out of the traffic jam of your life.

Lack of Knowledge—Many of us set out to accomplish a goal completely ignorant of what we need to do to get there. Everything in this book is related. If you go back to the chapters on establishing your goal, plans to achieve your goal, and doing all the right things to make sure you accomplish your goal, you will see that knowledge is such a vital part of making your goal a reality. Knowledge will allow you to realize whether you have the qualifications—physical, mental, financial, etc.—to get up and make it happen. Knowledge will direct your actions. Lack of knowledge will get you blindsided by events—events that, if you were aware of them from the beginning of your journey, would not catch you off guard and would not blindside you.

Until there is awareness, there can be no consensus for change. Let me say this again—until there is awareness, there can be no consensus for change; except maybe by accident, which is no way to live your life or the life you want for your family.

If you don't know that something is not good for you—if you don't know that the direction you are taking will not get you to your destination—you will continue along that direction to no avail. In other words, you won't do anything to fix it and you won't get there. You must first know that you are going in the wrong direction before you can fix anything—awareness is the key!

If you don't take the time to make yourself aware—if you don't take the time to study what it is that you want to accomplish—you will never know what it takes to get there. If we don't educate ourselves with the knowledge of how others accomplished what we are trying to do, we will most likely be caught off guard when there is really no reason for it. There is absolutely no reason to reinvent the wheel—to go through all the steps if some of the steps have already been done for you. You need to work smarter, not harder. But the only way to do this is to become more aware—aware of as many things as possible related to what you are trying to do. Because we lack the knowledge necessary to make informed decisions, we continue grasping at straws and going in the wrong direction.

Lack of Motivation—Maybe you just don't feel like doing what it takes to get what you want. Maybe you are tired or just feeling lazy. If this is you, you need to get real today—right now. A lot of us say we want to do something—become this significant person or become financially successful—but we aren't doing any of the things necessary to make these goals a reality. Some of us are just too busy—too busy having fun, watching TV, gossiping on the phone, or sleeping our life away. We are just too busy distracted with other stuff that we never find the time or motivation to do the hard work to move forward. We need to get motivated and this motivation has to come from within. We have to find that inner desire. Unfortunately—for many of us—that inner desire must be triggered by some significantly emotional experience. For example, the motivation to quit smoking may come from your having a stroke or heart attack—or from a loved one having a stroke or heart attack. In order to accomplish our goals, we need to find our inner desire to motivate ourselves right now.

PHYSICAL BARRIERS

Lack of Money—Do you lack the money necessary to accomplish your goals? Maybe you're experiencing extreme financial hardship. Do you feel like there's no way out of your financial hole? Well, there is a way—it's just that you don't realize it yet.

You're not the first person to experience financial difficulty, and I guarantee you that you will not be the last. Get educated on finances and budgeting issues today. Have you exhausted all the financial avenues available to you? What about attending free lectures and seminars in your local area—especially those put on by your local chamber of commerce and other civic organizations? Additionally, how do you personally define your local area?

Is it everything within ten miles, or can you expand your area to the next town or city? Can you expand your radius of action point to say, anything within forty miles from your home—or better yet, within a one-hour drive from your home? If you can do this, you will expose yourself to a much larger pool of financial resources and other networking opportunities that may provide you with excellent alternatives or options to finance your career or business venture. If your circle of friends, business associates, classmates, and people who want to achieve or make their life better by doing something about it is small, you can expect that your financial opportunities and options will also be small or nonexistent. If you do anything at all, expand your circle—you will be pleasantly surprised.

If you are not using the Internet to expand your circle, you are missing out on a truly valuable source of information—information from people all over the world. If you don't have a computer or access to the Internet, please visit your local library or maybe even get your job to allow you to have access to the Internet, especially if it gives them a better employee. Start talking to people who are financially successful and find a way to better your situation.

I am reminded here of a term I use often when talking with audiences—the term is Recognize, Relate, Assimilate, and Act (R^2A^2), taken from the book *The Science of Success* by Napoleon Hill—I paraphrase here for my purposes. *Recognize* opportunities when they reveal themselves to you—always be on the lookout and always be prepared for these opportunities. Then seriously *relate* yourself to this opportunity—ask yourself these relationship questions: Is this for me? Can I do this? Does this fit what I want to do? And next, I want you to *assimilate* someone or others in your area that are doing exactly what you are doing and are doing it very well. You can probably get them to mentor you and provide you insights as to how they achieved their goal. This can also be extended to people with fewer credentials or qualifications than you have, but nonetheless are very successful at doing what they want to do with their life. Study these folks and ask yourself—why are they successful?

Maybe it's because they have faith, maybe it's because they have desire; they have drive; they have motivation, and they believe in themselves. The last thing I want you to do is to *act* because if you don't act, the other steps don't matter—all you succeeded in doing is blowing smoke and doing nothing. You know the saying—talk is cheap!

Illness and Bad Health—Now, this is an interesting subject. What is bad health? Does bad health also include mental issues? Can an illness be mental? In this section, I want you to understand whether your health problem is a physical health issue or a mental health issue. And then you need to determine the impact these problems have on your ability to move forward with your goal. For example, if you are overweight, out of shape, or suffering from ill health, the first thing you should do is determine the root cause of the problem. With regards to being overweight, the problem could be caused by a bad diet, no exercise routine, a medical issue, or mentally you believe you can't change your situation. All of these areas should be addressed in order to overcome the problem. If you can't solve the situation yourself, then I advise you to seek professional help from a doctor, physical fitness coaches, personal trainers, psychiatrists, or the clergy. Research the appropriate medical care, if the problem is really a medical issue. If your problem is getting your body back in shape, research fitness coaches or personal trainers. If your problem is eating the wrong food at the wrong time, try consulting with a dietician. Or, after all the discussions above, is your health issue the result of a bigger issue like your motivation or lack thereof?

You need to ask yourself—what's driving your lack of motivation? Is your health a symptom of a much bigger problem? Whatever this bigger issue is, you need to really sit down and try to identify it immediately because until you determine what this bigger issue is, these health issues will continue to be a roadblock to achieving your goal or accomplishing whatever task is set before you.

Similarly, if your problem is a physical issue beyond your control that leaves you physically challenged, I definitely suggest seeking medical attention to help you to first cope with the challenge and accept it. I am absolutely amazed at folks who accept their physical challenges and go on to accomplish amazing things in their lives.

There is always someone worse off than you are—and I know that this is much easier said than done—but the fact remains that some of these folks are making it happen for themselves. I personally use them as a motivational jumpstart when I am feeling sorry for myself.

It is time to take control and realize that life can and must go on—so if you have the good fortune to continue to live, remember that time waits for no one. What better time than right now? Beethoven continued to compose beautiful music after he became deaf. He did not allow physical disability to stop him from accomplishing his goals. If he did not—neither should you!

Stop! Take time out and make a list of the things that are stopping you from accomplishing your goals.

1.

2.

3.

4.

5.

6.

7.

8.

9.

10.

Ask yourself—what is it that you can do today to overcome the mental and physical barriers standing between you and your goals?

1.

2.

3.

4.

5.

6.

7.

8.

9.

10.

CHAPTER 11

DON'T GIVE UP!

D on't give up! Don't give up in your personal life and don't give up in your business life. Any goal you have that you want to accomplish is going to have some obstacles. Sometimes you're going to be stuck in traffic, feeling like you're going nowhere fast. But you can't give up. Sometimes you're going to be going in the wrong direction and end up farther from your goal than when you first set out on your journey. But you can't give up. Sometimes it will look like everybody is against you—no one believes in you and the winds of good fortune are not blowing your way. But even then, you can't give up.

Henry Ford—one of America's greatest inventors—didn't give up. He spent most of his money, time, and energy perfecting the Model T. He went home at night with the Model T on his mind. He dismantled the Ford over and over and over again in his quest for perfecting the automobile. The people around him were astonished and amazed at his desire to be the best and some even thought he was too ambitious—maybe a little crazy. But look—today, Ford is still around. Because Henry Ford did not give up in his pursuit to be the best that he could be, the Ford car is still one of the best-selling automobiles in the world.

No matter what, you need to persist—you need to continue to press on; don't give up. Don't let minor or major setbacks stop you. Don't allow failures to discourage you. Most millionaires declared bankruptcy before achieving success, and many of them did this more than a few times. Donald Trump immediately comes to mind. He has declared bankruptcy several times but has never given up. During this book's rewrite, he is still a multimillionaire and currently running for president of the United States as the presumptive Republican nominee—where he is funding his entire campaign without financial assistance from others. In my opinion, Trump believes that he can win at whatever he wants to do and spends his energy on winning, no matter what noise surrounds him. Shut your ears to those negative people who tell you that you can't achieve your goal. They will kick you when you're down and love you when you are up.

Like you, many have faced what seemed like obstacles so big that they could not overcome them. I remember when I first arrived at Tuskegee University to pursue my engineering degree. I was confident, proud, knew that I could do well. I knew that I was at my best, having graduated in the top 5 percent of my senior class from John's Island, South Carolina. My goodness, I was voted "Best All Around" by my senior classmates—they believed I had all the right stuff to be successful. I was confident that I could accomplish anything.

As it turned out, however, I wasn't as prepared as I thought. I was really a little old country boy from the South and educated in the South. I hate to knock the South—remember, this was 1972—but a lot of the students in my Tuskegee University engineering class were from the northern states, and most of them had already taken college-level math, which included calculus. Well, little old country-boy me did not have any of these classes in my high school, and if we did, I surely didn't take advantage of any of these advanced classes.

I was behind, and not just behind white students, but behind other black students as well—black students from the North and black students from the South who were made aware early in their education process to take the right college preparatory courses. This was very frustrating for me. I had not studied what it took to become an engineer, so I had not taken the math classes necessary to move forward in my engineering studies immediately after arriving at college. So while I was busy playing catch-up and taking prerequisite entry-level math courses, my peers—I always considered myself in the top 5 percent—were on the fast track to getting their engineering degree in four years versus the five-year schedule I was on. Some were even taking calculus the first semester of our freshman year.

My ego was crushed. I felt crippled. The math classes I took in my first year didn't count toward my degree. The classes counted toward total college credits, but they didn't do anything for my mechanical engineering major.

I was discouraged. I could have given up. I could have changed majors, which was very tempting considering several of my classmates did just that. I could have said, "This isn't fair. I give up." But I didn't. And because I didn't give up, I caught up with my peers, worked hard, stayed focused on my goal, and received my mechanical engineering degree—graduating *cum laude* in the top 5 percent of my class.

When life hits you with obstacles and when you suffer from the consequences of not being prepared, you can't just stay down and cry—you have to get up and stay focused on your goal. Stay focused on the reason you are where you are and do the necessary things to finish what you started. I did and so can you!

DO YOU FEEL LIKE GIVING UP?

Before you throw your hands up and throw the towel in, ask yourself the following questions:

Have you done your homework? Did you study your goal thoroughly? If you haven't done your homework on your goal, then you have not given yourself a fighting chance—and you are cheating yourself if you give up now. Look at your goals and ask yourself if you have thoroughly investigated what you say you want to do.

Have you followed your plan? Did you do everything in your power to accomplish your goal? Be honest. If your goal is to lose weight, did you exercise every day and eat healthy food? No guesswork. If you followed the instructions from earlier, you know that you need to keep track of what it is that you're doing on a daily basis to accomplish your goals. Keeping a written record of your activities keeps you honest. If you haven't done everything in your power to accomplish your goal, then *you don't have the right to give up.*

Have you given yourself enough time to accomplish your goal? How long did it take others to accomplish the thing that you are trying to achieve? Learn patience and be realistic in what you can accomplish in any given amount of time.

MAKING AN INFORMED DECISION ON GIVING UP

In my opinion, the only valid reason for giving up is that you lack desire. Maybe you don't really want what it is that you say you want to accomplish. Go back and think about what your motivation is for pursuing your goal. Are you motivated by love? Or are you motivated by fear, money, fame, or power? Only desire or love can get you through the hard times of this life journey.

If you don't have love for what you are doing, you're going to give up. If you are pursuing a goal only because you think you can make a lot of money, you're going to give up. Get real about your motivation, and if you realize that you do have love for the thing that you are trying to accomplish, then you should not give up.

You should not give up until you've exhausted all avenues— and even then, you need to give it a second and thorough thought.

When life's darkest moments descend upon you, don't give up.

When you think life is over, don't give up.

In many cases, the only way to lose at something is to quit.

Don't quit. Don't give up. Do the following:

Stop! Take the time to analyze your situation and answer the following questions:

If you feel like giving up, what are your reasons for feeling this way?

1.

2.

3.

4.

5.

6.

7.

8.

9.

10.

What are the things that you *haven't* done that you should have done in the pursuit of your goal?

1.

2.

3.

4.

5.

6.

7.

8.

9.

10.

For the things that you haven't done that you should have done in the pursuit of your goals, take the time now to figure out a plan to do those things before you consider giving up. Tell yourself why you haven't done what it takes to accomplish your goals and create a simple and measurable way to implement those actions into your plan.

In a world where most people just go with the flow, never challenging the tide, it can be difficult to walk to the beat of your own drummer. But for those who dare to move confidently in the direction of their dreams, there is a treasure awaiting you—not of gold or silver; but of happiness and a life fully lived.

DON'T GIVE UP!

CONCLUSION

If you find that your life resembles being stuck in traffic, I hope that by reading this book, you find a way to get yourself unstuck—and most of all, a means to avoid getting stuck in the future. I hope that your life has been touched in some way—that you can identify with some of the chapter content—and that I have inspired you to start right now to make a positive difference in your life.

Read and discuss *Are You Stuck in Traffic?* with your significant other, your family, and your friends.

Additionally—in Appendix A—a one-page, stand-alone handout modified from my motivational TV series presentations is provided for each chapter discussed in this book.

Appendix B provides additional information about The Saunders Executive Resources Group, LLC, sample seminar sessions, and a couple of homework assignments for those of you who want or need extra credit.

It has been my pleasure!

Dr. William R. Saunders
Colonel, USAF Retired

MOTIVATIONAL SERIES: ARE YOU STUCK IN TRAFFIC?—AN INTERESTING PARALLEL TO LIFE? AN INTERACTIVE APPROACH

Description: Series of questions designed to provoke thought; to provoke action; to get you prepared for contingencies. Designed as a five-minute teaser discussion—interactive, motivational, and provocative.

- Have you ever been stuck in traffic and going nowhere?
- What about with your life? Your goals? Your plans? Your education? Your dreams?
- What does "stuck in traffic" mean to you?
  - Same old job / relationship / routine / situation / etc.
- Why are you stuck in traffic? Do you get stuck often? Are your friends stuck?
- Have you been stuck in traffic long? Do you care?
- Did you plan for it? Did you anticipate the traffic?
- What happens when you get stuck?
- Do you have a course of action? Do you have a plan?
- Have you done a cost-benefit analysis?
- Do you get frustrated?
- What is available to ease your frustration?

THINGS YOU CAN DO:

- Pull out pen and paper and take an inventory of your life right now.
- Determine what has you stuck in traffic.

- What can you change to prevent being stuck?
- What are some of the things you can do to avoid getting stuck?
- What are some of the things you can do when you find yourself stuck?
- Improve your position.
  - Know your priorities—do your homework, be early, study.
  - Go back to school / take a vacation / relax / read a book / find a trade / etc.
  - Let others help you.
- Brainstorm all available options for before, during, and after being stuck in life's traffic.

Stop for a moment and analyze your situation. If you take the time to analyze your life, you may find that you can minimize being stuck in the traffic of life. This one-page handout by Dr. William Saunders is provided for your use as a handy, stand-alone, quick-reference guide to make you think. There are no right or wrong answers and no judgment. Find ways to "unstuck" yourself today—life is too precious to be stuck in traffic!

Objectives:

1. Readers learn how to start the process of getting their life in order.
2. Readers learn how to anticipate/prepare for things that cause them to be stuck in traffic.

Website: http://thesaundersexecutiveresourcesgroup.com; Email: bill.saunders@cox.net

MEMBER

NATIONAL SPEAKERS ASSOCIATION

Certified 8(a) BD, Small Disadvantage Business (SDB), Service-Disabled Veteran-Owned Business (SDVOB)
Formerly Showcased: *Forbes*, *Business Week* and *The* AtlantaBizJournals Online Magazines
© William R. Saunders, 2017, Macon, GA

MOTIVATIONAL SERIES: ARE YOU THE BEST AT WHAT YOU DO? IF NOT, WHY NOT, AND WHAT ARE YOU GOING TO DO ABOUT IT?—AN INTERACTIVE APPROACH

Description: Series of comments and questions designed to provoke thought; to provoke action; to get you prepared for contingencies. Designed as a five-minute teaser discussion—interactive, motivational, and provocative.

- If you are the best, what are you doing to stay the best?
- Define the word "best." Are you number one? Do you care?
- If you are not the best, what are you doing to make yourself the best?
- Do you need to go back to school? Do you need to go to training schools?
- Do you know where you are right now?
- What are you doing about it? Who can you turn to? Who can help make a difference?
- Are you the best worker? Are you the best employee?
- What do you need to do to improve your position? To get you on the right track?
- Are you prepared to make yourself the best? Are you educating yourself?
- Are you talking to your friends? Are your friends helping you?
- Are you going back to school? Are you doing your homework? Studying?
- What is your motivation for being the best? Do you really want to be the best?

- Where do you want to be in the grand scheme of things?
- Are you not motivated? Are you doing this for yourself? For someone else?

THINGS YOU CAN DO:

- You need to get yourself mentally prepared to be the best—whatever that is.
- Know yourself and your capabilities, know your strengths, know your weaknesses.
- Know thy enemies, know thyself—in most cases, you are your worst enemy.
- Know the people closest to you are the ones who stop you from achieving your best.
- Determine who is on your side and who is not.
- Take the time to make yourself the best at whatever you want to be.
- Take advantage of what's available to allow you to achieve your best.
- It's time to stop all the excuses—all the reasons why you can't do something.
- Know the things that are within your control (like studying, attitude, etc.).

Stop for a moment and analyze your situation—find ways to make yourself the best today! This one-page handout by Dr. William Saunders is provided for your use as a handy, stand-alone, quick-reference guide to make you think. There are no right or wrong answers and no judgment—just be the best at what you do.

Objectives:

1. Readers learn how to start the process of making themselves the best at what they do.
2. Readers learn how to anticipate and prepare for things that impact their lives.

Website: http://thesaundersexecutiveresourcesgroup.com;
Email: bill.saunders@cox.net

MEMBER

NATIONAL SPEAKERS ASSOCIATION

Certified 8(a) BD, Small Disadvantage Business (SDB), Service-Disabled Veteran-Owned Business
(SDVOB)
Formerly Showcased: *Forbes*, *Business Week* and *The* AtlantaBizJournals Online Magazines
© William R. Saunders, 2017, Macon, GA

MOTIVATIONAL SERIES: WHAT IS YOUR GOAL, YOUR STARTING POINT? CONNECT THE TWO; BELIEVE IT AND YOU CAN ACHIEVE IT—AN INTERACTIVE APPROACH

Description: Series of comments and questions designed to provoke thought; to provoke action; to get you prepared for contingencies. Designed as a five-minute teaser discussion—interactive, motivational, and provocative.

- What is your goal? Is it your goal? Is it someone else's goal?
- Where is your starting point? Where are you right now?
- Is your goal realistic? Achievable? Is it doable? Does it make sense to you?
- Are you qualified?
- What are the roadblocks to achieving your goal? Are they money? Time? Others?
- Can you move these roadblocks? Do you need help moving these roadblocks?
- Do you believe you can achieve this goal? Do you understand the goal?
- Are you prepared to do what it takes to achieve your goal?
- What are the things you need to do to make yourself qualified?
- Are you motivated? Are you tired?
- Are you procrastinating? Are you sitting on yesterday's wins?
- Do you have clarity of purpose with your life?

THINGS YOU CAN DO:

- Find a quiet spot and brainstorm what your goal is—know your goal today.
- Share your goal with your significant other/trusted friend and solicit support.
- Write down the things you need to do, in chronological order, to make the goal a reality.
- Make sure you know where your starting point is, and then connect to your end point.
- Seriously ask yourself if you truly believe that you can achieve this goal.
- Stay focused on your goal—get rid of the things that hinder you from achieving the goal.

It's time to have a goal that is realistic and achievable. Stop for a moment and analyze your goal—is it still realistic given today's technology and relationships? This one-page handout by Dr. William Saunders is provided for your use as a handy, stand-alone, quick-reference guide to make you think. There are no right or wrong answers and no judgment. Define your goal today.

Objectives:

1. Readers learn how to start the process of defining their goal.
2. Readers learn how to anticipate and prepare for things that impact their lives.

Website: http://thesaundersexecutiveresourcesgroup.com;
Email: bill.saunders@cox.net

MEMBER

NATIONAL SPEAKERS ASSOCIATION

Certified 8(a) BD, Small Disadvantage Business (SDB), Service-Disabled Veteran-Owned Business (SDVOB)
Formerly Showcased: *Forbes*, *Business Week* and *The* AtlantaBizJournals Online Magazines
© William R. Saunders, 2017, Macon, GA

MOTIVATIONAL SERIES: WHAT IS YOUR PLAN TO ACHIEVE YOUR GOAL? IS IT REALISTIC? IS IT YOUR PLAN?—AN INTERACTIVE APPROACH

Description: Series of questions designed to provoke thought; to provoke action; to get you prepared for contingencies. Designed as a five-minute teaser discussion—interactive, motivational, and provocative.

- Do you have a plan? Where is it? When is the last time you looked at your plan?
- Is it your plan? Is it someone else's plan? Is the plan normal for you?
- Can you achieve the actions designed by the plan?
- If you don't have a plan, what are you doing to put your plan to action?
- Do you have a backup plan?
- What are the steps? How many steps?
- Is your plan in line with your goals?
- Is your plan prioritized? How many things are on your plate?
- What things can come off your plate?
- What are the competing tasks? Which task comes first? How many tasks are there?
- What is your motivation to achieve your plan?

THINGS YOU CAN DO:

- Relate your plan to others doing what you want to do and doing it well.
- Do your homework.
- Make sure your plan makes sense for you, especially as it relates to your goal.

- Don't sugarcoat what you want to do—don't pacify yourself.
- Believe in the plan; believe in yourself—act now to put a plan in place.
- Modify the plan as required.

It's time to put a plan of action in place! This one-page handout by Dr. William Saunders is provided for your use as a handy, stand-alone, quick reference guide to make you think. There are no right or wrong answers and no judgment. Put together a plan that allows you to achieve your goal.

Objectives:

1. Readers learn how to start the process of putting a plan of action in place.
2. Readers understand the importance of having a plan to achieve their goal.

Website: http://thesaundersexecutiveresourcesgroup.com;
Email: bill.saunders@cox.net

MEMBER

Certified 8(a) BD, Small Disadvantage Business (SDB), Service-Disabled Veteran-Owned Business (SDVOB)
Formerly Showcased: *Forbes*, *Business Week* and *The* AtlantaBizJournals Online Magazines
© William R. Saunders, 2017, Macon, GA

MOTIVATIONAL SERIES: ARE YOU PREPARED TO TELL ME WHO YOU ARE IN THIRTY SECONDS? AN INTERACTIVE APPROACH

Description: Series of questions designed to provoke thought; to provoke action; to get you prepared for contingencies. Designed as a five-minute teaser discussion—interactive, motivational, and provocative.

- Do you know who you are? Can you tell me who you are in thirty seconds?
- What value do you bring to the table?
- Why should I hire you over someone else?
- What makes you so different?
- Can you articulate/communicate what you have provided on paper? Not on paper?
  - o 100 candidates, three jobs—you made top 10 percent but all paperwork looks the same
  - o Authority figures don't have time to read but will make a decision
  - o If called, do you already know what you want to say?
  - o Can you communicate succinctly, specifically, and quantifiably who you are?
- Can you market yourself in thirty seconds?
- Why should a potential client purchase your product, your service, or hire you?
- Tell me right now—you have thirty seconds, so don't waste it.
- Did this question or questions catch you off-guard? If it did, Why? What does this mean?

THINGS YOU CAN DO:

- Don't allow yourself to be caught off guard.
- Always anticipate this question.
- Practice, practice, practice until you get it just right—make it second nature.
- Practice in front of the mirror, your kids, your friends, your spouse.
- Make sure you are prepared.
- Do your homework.
- Analyze your audience—potential client, customer, employer, etc.
- Get yourself ready.

Make sure you can tell people who you are without mistakes. This one-page handout by Dr. William Saunders is provided for your use as a handy, stand-alone, quick-reference guide to make you think. There are no right or wrong answers and no judgment. Can you tell me who you are in thirty seconds?

Objectives:

1. Readers learn self-confidence and how to prioritize.
2. Readers learn significance of not being caught off guard. of being prepared.

Website: http://thesaundersexecutiveresourcesgroup.com;
Email: bill.saunders@cox.net

MEMBER

NATIONAL SPEAKERS ASSOCIATION

Certified 8(a) BD, Small Disadvantage Business (SDB), Service-Disabled Veteran-Owned Business (SDVOB)
Formerly Showcased: *Forbes*, *Business Week* and *The* AtlantaBizJournals Online Magazines
© William R. Saunders, 2017, Macon, GA

MOTIVATIONAL SERIES: SO YOU ARE TOO BUSY—TELL ME WHY YOU ARE SO BUSY—AN INTERACTIVE APPROACH

Description: Series of questions designed to provoke thought; to provoke action; to get you prepared for contingencies. Designed as a five-minute teaser discussion—interactive, motivational, and provocative.

- Why are you so busy? What makes you so busy?
- Who are you that your life is so busy you can't respond to something within twenty-four to forty-eight hours?
- Who is controlling your time?
- Are you spending too much time doing nonproductive things during the day?
- Have you dissected your day? What do you do all day? What are you doing right now?
- What are your priorities? What are your needs? What are your wants?
- Is your life in balance? How do you put it all in balance?
- What are the things that can be eliminated? How much time do you gain?
- Are you volunteering too much of your services? How many outside organizations?
- Are you too busy to go back to school? To get a certificate, training?
- Are you too busy to put your life in order? In balance? Too busy to play with the kids?
- Are you too busy to take your spouse/significant other to lunch or dinner?

THINGS YOU CAN DO:

- Take an inventory of your life right now.
- Pull out pen and paper and write down everything you do each day.
- Brainstorm this list—don't try to analyze this list right now, just get it down on paper.
- Don't shortchange yourself, either—include everything you do.
- Prioritize this list into MUST DO (Needs) and WOULD LIKE TO DO (Wants).
- Now take a look at what can be eliminated or moved to another day.

Stop for a moment and analyze your situation—if you take the time to analyze your life, you may find that you can make the time to take care of you, your family, etc. Life is too short to be so busy every day of the week. Take something off your plate today. Learn how to say no when and where you can! This one-page handout by Dr. William Saunders is provided for your use as a handy, stand-alone, quick-reference guide to make you think. There are no right or wrong answers and no judgment. Stop being so busy!

Objectives:

1. Readers learn the importance of prioritizing activities that impact their lives.
2. Readers learn the significance of Time Management.

Website: http://thesaundersexecutiveresourcesgroup.com;
Email: bill.saunders@cox.net

MEMBER

NATIONAL SPEAKERS ASSOCIATION

Certified 8(a) BD, Small Disadvantage Business (SDB), Service-Disabled Veteran-Owned Business (SDVOB)

Formerly Showcased: *Forbes*, *Business Week* and *The* AtlantaBizJournals Online Magazines

© William R. Saunders, 2017, Macon, GA

MOTIVATIONAL SERIES: IT'S TIME TO GET UP—NOT LATER, BUT RIGHT NOW!—AN INTERACTIVE APPROACH

Description: Series of questions designed to provoke thought; to provoke action; to get you prepared for contingencies. Designed as a five-minute teaser discussion—interactive, motivational, and provocative.

- Why are you still sitting down when you have things to do?
- Are you not motivated? Are you tired? What is it?
- It's time to get up—no more procrastination; no more sitting on yesterday's wins.
- It's time to make that goal a reality—it's time to act; it's time to execute.
- It's time to have clarity of purpose with your life—read the book *The Purpose-Driven Life.*
- It's time to make yourself the best at what you do.
- It's time to rise above being just okay.
- It's time to make yourself stand out—in the workplace, in class; be the best.
- It's time to go back to school if you need to.
- It's time to stop going in the wrong direction—especially when you know it.
- If you are going in the wrong direction with your life, your family, your career, your job, your children, your health, your friends—you need to stop right now.
- The goal that you want will not be achieved if you continue along this path.

- You need to change direction and you need to do it today—right now.
- It's time to put your life in order—it's time to take inventory of your life.
- It's time to get rid of those excess things that take you away from achieving your goal—those friends, things that bring you no value.
- It's time to stop all the excuses—all the reasons why you can't do something.
- It's time to take care of those things that are within your control.
- It's time to look at how to make things happen and stop looking at how not to.
- If there is a 1 percent chance of making it happen, put your energy in this 1 percent.
- It's time to stop wasting your time with the 95 percent naysayers—work with the 5 percent.
- It's time to put balance in your life—it's time to know and take care of your priorities.

It's time to get up! Stop for a moment and analyze your habits—are you sitting down on the job? Your life? Well, if you are—stop it! Don't shortchange your life or your family—make the changes; get up right now and live your life the way it should be lived. Put your life in balance. This one-page handout by Dr. William Saunders is provided for your use as a handy, stand-alone, quick-reference guide to make you think. There are no right or wrong answers and no judgment. Get up and act right now!

Objectives:

1. Readers learn how to start the process of getting the maximum benefits out of life.
2. Readers learn how to anticipate and prepare for things that impact their lives.

Website: http://thesaundersexecutiveresourcesgroup.com;
Email: bill.saunders@cox.net

MEMBER

NATIONAL SPEAKERS ASSOCIATION

Certified 8(a) BD, Small Disadvantage Business (SDB), Service-Disabled Veteran-Owned Business
(SDVOB)
Formerly Showcased: *Forbes*, *Business Week* and *The* AtlantaBizJournals Online Magazines
© William R. Saunders, 2017, Macon, GA

MOTIVATIONAL SERIES: WHAT'S STOPPING YOU FROM ACHIEVING YOUR GOAL?—IDENTIFYING THE THINGS WITHIN YOUR CONTROL!—AN INTERACTIVE APPROACH

Description: Series of questions designed to provoke thought; to provoke action; to get you prepared for contingencies. Designed as a five-minute teaser discussion—interactive, motivational, and provocative.

- Do you know what's stopping you from achieving your goals? Do you care?
- What are the roadblocks to achieving your goal?
- What is your economic status? Do you care? Can you do something about it?
- How is the job market where you live? Can you get the right job? Why not?
- Is education holding you back? Do you need to go back to school?
- Have you truly taken the time to evaluate the roadblocks to achieving your goal?
- Is your attitude the problem? What about your friend's attitude? Your family's?
- Are you motivated? Are you tired? What is it? Do you get enough rest?
- Is it your health? Are you physically and mentally able to achieve the goal?
- Are you procrastinating on your own, or is someone else causing the procrastination?
- Have you analyzed your life for the moment, the day, the week—the rest of your life?

- Why don't you or can't you control the things within your control?

THINGS YOU CAN DO:

- Identify the things stopping you from achieving, no matter how small.
- Take charge—identify those things within your control and take care of them.
- Use the things within your control to your advantage, not to your disadvantage.
- Solicit feedback from a friend, a coworker, a teacher, a supervisor.
- Seek wise counsel, if required.
- Take inventory of your life and get rid of those excess things that bring you no value.
- It's time to stop all the excuses—all the reasons why you can't do something.

Take charge of your life! Do it today—right now. Don't shortchange your life or your family; be responsible for the things within your control—make the changes right now that will put you on the right track to achieving your goal. This one-page handout by Dr. William Saunders is provided for your use as a handy, stand-alone, quick-reference guide to make you think. There are no right or wrong answers and no judgment. Identify and eliminate the roadblocks in your life today.

Objectives:

1. Readers learn how to start the process of taking charge of their destiny.
2. Readers learn how to identify roadblocks to achieving their goal.

Website: http://thesaundersexecutiveresourcesgroup.com;
Email: bill.saunders@cox.net

MEMBER

Certified 8(a) BD, Small Disadvantage Business (SDB), Service-Disabled Veteran-Owned Business (SDVOB)
Formerly Showcased: *Forbes*, *Business Week* and *T*he AtlantaBizJournals Online Magazines

MOTIVATIONAL SERIES: DON'T GIVE UP!—AN INTERACTIVE APPROACH

Description: Series of questions designed to provoke thought; to provoke action; to get you prepared for contingencies. Designed as a five-minute teaser discussion—interactive, motivational, and provocative.

- What exactly is the definition of giving up?
    - o Does it mean to quit, to stop, to fall down, to give in (in life and in business)?
- Do you give up when you still have the ability to make it?
- Do you give up when you still have time to get it right—to get on track?
- When should you give up? At what point should you give up?
    - o Is it after exhausting all the facts?
    - o Is it after doing everything within your power, within your control?
        - ▪ Do you know what's within your control?
    - o Is it after doing all the right things? After analyzing your situation?
    - o Is it after adding up all the pluses and minuses?
    - o Is it after some serious soul searching, attitude check, gut check?
    - o Is it after realizing that doing all of the above still results in failure?

THINGS YOU CAN DO:

- Pause, think, yield, take a time-out, hack the clock, wait a minute.
- Consider why you are quitting. Consider why you are giving up.
- Is it because you should not have started? Did you start with the right motivation?
- If you don't have to make the decision to quit today, don't make it.
    - Make sure you know how much time is left (days, weeks, months, etc.).
    - Make sure you know your limitations.
- Make sure you are prepared—what are the things you need to get prepared?
- Study, do your homework, stay physically and mentally fit, stay healthy and rest.
- Don't give up before exhausting all avenues available—and I mean all avenues.
- Every day you get up brings you something; make sure you get this new something!

Stop, think, and analyze your situation thoroughly. If you can just wait a moment, life might just surprise you. This one-page handout by Dr. William Saunders is provided for your use as a handy, stand-alone, quick-reference guide to make you think. There are no right or wrong answers and no judgment. Don't give up!

Objectives:

1. Readers learn to process all information before making decisions to quit.
2. Readers learn the importance of making a timely, wise decision.

Website: http://thesaundersexecutiveresourcesgroup.com;
Email: bill.saunders@cox.net

MEMBER

NATIONAL SPEAKERS ASSOCIATION

Certified 8(a) BD, Small Disadvantage Business (SDB), Service-Disabled Veteran-Owned Business (SDVOB)
Formerly Showcased: *Forbes*, *Business Week* and *T*he AtlantaBizJournals Online Magazines

Join **Colonel Bill Saunders** for a **Powerful Motivational Seminar.**

IMPRESSION MANAGEMENT
Marketing Yourself, Your Business, Your Relationships

If you are not where you want to be, this seminar is for you. If you are interested in "Managing the Impression" you leave with others the very first time, this seminar is for you. If you want that great job, that big promotion, this seminar is for you.

ONLY 40 SEATS AVAILABLE! To reserve your space now call **478-320-9172**
or email: Bill.Saunders@cox.net

Group Discounts Available
*Payment required 2 days prior to each session in order to reserve a seat. Cash or check, please.

May 23
6:30 p.m.
Tuesday

Location:
Holiday Inn, Macon West
Executive Room
4755 Chambers Road
Macon, GA 31206

(I-475 & Eisenhower Parkway)

*Visit www.TheSaundersExecutiveResourcesGroup.com

Designed by Reggie Saunders Designs
www.ReggieSaundersDesigns.com

Join **Colonel Bill Saunders** for a **Powerful Motivational Seminar.**

The **Saunders**
Executive Resources Group,LLC.

━━━━ The Art of ━━━━
Public Speaking

The Unspoken or Spoken Word--What Does It Mean?

If you want to improve your ability to communicate
succinctly, without hesitation, your product, service, or just
who you are from a business or personal perspective to
one person or five hundred, this seminar is for you.

ONLY 40 SEATS AVAILABLE! To reserve your
space now call **478-320-9172**
or email: Bill.Saunders@cox.net

Group Discounts Available
*Payment required 2 days prior to each session
in order to reserve a seat. Cash or check, please.

Jun 27
6:30 p.m.
Tuesday
Location:
Holiday Inn, Macon West
Executive Room
4755 Chambers Road
Macon, GA 31206

(I-475
&
Eisenhower
Parkway)

*Visit www.TheSaundersExecutiveResourcesGroup.com

Designed by Reggie Saunders Designs
www.ReggieSaundersDesigns.com

Join **Colonel Bill Saunders** for a **Powerful Motivational Seminar.**

The Art of Exceptional

Customer Service

Building Relationships that Last!!

Customer Service is the number one priority of any business, and yet it appears lacking wherever we go. If you are interested in providing great customer service every time, this seminar is for you.

ONLY 40 SEATS AVAILABLE! Call

(478) 320-9172 or purchase tickets **ONLINE** at
www.TheSaundersExecutiveResourcesGroup.com

Group Discounts Available

*Payment required 2 days prior to each session in order to reserve a seat. Cash or check, please.

Jul 25

6:30 p.m.
Tuesday
Location:
Holiday Inn, Macon West
Executive Room
4755 Chambers Road
Macon, GA 31206

(I-475 & Eisenhower Parkway)

email: Bill.Saunders@cox.net

For information regarding lectures, workshops, seminars, keynotes, or ordering books, audio CDs, or DVDS by the author, please visit my website, call, e-mail, or write:

Dr. William R. Saunders, Colonel, USAF Retired
P.O. Box 26095
Macon GA 31221
Email: bill.saunders@cox.net
478-320-9172

Website:
http://www.TheSaundersExecutiveResourcesGroup.com

HOMEWORK

FOR NETWORKING PURPOSES, PROVIDE A LIST OF
PEOPLE YOU KNOW WHO DON'T KNOW YOU:

1.

2.

3.

4.

5.

6.

7.

8.

9.

10.

HOMEWORK CONTINUED

NOW, PROVIDE A LIST OF PEOPLE WHO KNOW YOU OR WHO YOU WANT TO KNOW WHO CAN MAKE A DIFFERENCE IN YOUR LIFE (e.g. president, mayor, CEO, GM, senior management, secretary, pastor, commander, colonel, associate, relatives, etc.):

1.

2.

3.

4.

5.

6.

7.

8.

9.

10.

NOTES

Dr. William R. Saunders (Colonel, USAF Retired) is currently president and managing member of The Saunders Executive Resources Group, LLC, a service-disabled veteran-owned small business. He is a native of John's Island, South Carolina, where he graduated from St. John's High School in 1972. Dr. Saunders is a graduate of Tuskegee University, Tuskegee, Alabama, with a bachelor's degree in mechanical engineering (*cum laude*), a master's degree in business administration from Golden Gate University, San Francisco, California, a master of science degree in national resource strategy from the Industrial College of the Armed Forces, Ft. Lesly J. McNair, Washington, DC, and a doctorate in business administration from Argosy University, Atlanta, Georgia.

Dr. Saunders is a nationally known motivational speaker, educator, and professional development–training consultant. He is a professional member of the National Speakers Association (NSA) and has been on the national speaking circuit since 2005, conducting keynotes, workshops, and seminars throughout the United States. With over thirty-four years of proven leadership, Dr. Saunders has inspired thousands to make a positive difference in their lives with his message of self-empowerment. Through his thought-provoking, participatory, interactive, and conversational style, he implores his listeners to dive deep into their psyche in a quest to uncover the root of their problems and to shed light on how to improve their life's journey.

Dr. Saunders is a command pilot with more than 3,200 flight hours, a decorated Desert Storm veteran with fifty-seven flying missions, a former assistant professor at Howard University, and has held several high-level operational positions at the Pentagon in Washington, DC, and served as both the inspector general and director of Readiness and Homeland Security at the Warner Robins Air Logistics Center, the largest employer in the state of Georgia. Additionally, Dr. Saunders is the former chief administrative officer (CAO)/city manager for the great city of Macon, Georgia.